William Scribner

The Saviour's Converts

what we owe to them, and how we may aid them

William Scribner

The Saviour's Converts
what we owe to them, and how we may aid them

ISBN/EAN: 9783337313937

Printed in Europe, USA, Canada, Australia, Japan

Cover: Foto ©Lupo / pixelio.de

More available books at **www.hansebooks.com**

THE
SAVIOUR'S CONVERTS

THE

SAVIOUR'S CONVERTS

WHAT WE OWE TO THEM, AND HOW WE MAY AID THEM

BY THE

REV. WILLIAM SCRIBNER

AUTHOR OF

"PRAY FOR THE HOLY SPIRIT," "THESE LITTLE ONES," ETC.

"We cannot but think that this whole subject of the spiritual care, nurture, and training of young disciples, deserves to be more fully considered, and practically to be brought into far greater prominence."—RAY PALMER.

NEW YORK
CHARLES SCRIBNER'S SONS
743 AND 745 BROADWAY
1880

COPYRIGHT BY
CHARLES SCRIBNER'S SONS.
1880.

TROW'S
PRINTING AND BOOKBINDING COMPANY,
201-213 *East 12th Street*,
NEW YORK.

PREFATORY NOTE.

THIS little book was written not so much to call the attention of the *Church* to the duty of which it treats, as for the purpose of deepening the interest which all Christians take in converts, and of inciting the members of our churches to increased efforts to benefit them. There are portions of the volume, as the third and fourth chapters, which the writer ventures to hope may be read with profit by the convert himself.

CONTENTS.

CHAPTER I.
PAGE

Converts—The Holy Spirit's Agency—Revivals—The Religious Experience of Converts...................... 1

CHAPTER II.

Inducements which should stimulate the People of God to engage in the Work of helping Converts............. 32

CHAPTER III.

Some of the doctrinal Truths which the Convert should be assisted to apprehend clearly, in order that he may have a healthy Religious Experience, and also grow in Grace... 64

CHAPTER IV.

Some of the Christian's Duties, Difficulties, Privileges, and Activities, in regard to which the Convert needs to be Instructed 104

CHAPTER V.

From the earliest Times special Attention has been given by the Church to Catechizing the Young............ 154

THE SAVIOUR'S CONVERTS.

CHAPTER I.

CONVERTS—THE HOLY SPIRIT'S AGENCY—REVIVALS —THE RELIGIOUS EXPERIENCE OF CONVERTS.

THE vigor of the spiritual life, and the strength of the faith of some converts, have attracted the attention of the whole Church. Not all those who in primitive times suffered tortures and death rather than deny the Saviour were mature Christians. Many of them were converts. It is interesting to know this. In various periods, and in many places where the standard of the cross has been planted, the Church has had her martyrs, and of these none have been more steadfast than new disciples. Young maidens like Blandina, mere boys like Ponticus, cheerfully, nay triumphantly, bore tortures rather than deny their Lord. Churches established in our own times by the labors of missionaries have often been severely persecuted, but none of the members of these churches have endured persecution at the hands of their heathen countrymen with greater constancy than young converts.

But although piety and devotion to the Saviour and His cause have been very remarkable in the case of many converts, yet it is not to be expected that, as a general rule, young disciples will be strong and well established in the faith. They greatly need the sympathy and assistance of their brethren who are more advanced, and it is our design in writing this little book to incite our readers to do all in their power to aid them.

Some are of opinion that of the number who have recently begun the Christian course only those born outside of the Church can, with strict propriety of speech, be called converts. They doubt whether those should be considered accessions to the Church who are born and bred within her pale. We intend, however, to apply the word converts to all who have only been the professed followers of the Saviour for a short time, whether, as children of the covenant, they were born within the visible Church, or whether they had been outside of the Church until they, in their own persons, professed repentance and faith. Many belonging to this latter class are old in years, while considered as members of the Saviour's Church they are young. "I am just four years old," said a man of fourscore, as he leaned on his hoe in the garden. "Four years ago I began to serve God, and then I began to live."

We wish in this chapter to show briefly, 1. That it belongs to the Holy Spirit alone to make converts. 2. That although none are true converts except those whom the Holy Spirit has made such, many regard themselves as converts who have never been the subjects of the Spirit's saving work, and who are therefore self-deceived. 3. That souls may be converted, and are in fact constantly converted, at other times than in revivals. But 4. That countless numbers of converts are the fruits of revivals. And 5. That different converts vary as to their exercises.

1. *It belongs to the Holy Spirit alone to make converts.*

This will be evident, in the first place, when we consider that it is by being regenerated that one becomes a convert, that is, turns from sin unto God, and that regeneration is that instantaneous change from spiritual death to spiritual life of which the soul is the subject when the Holy Spirit creates it anew by a single exertion of His power.

If no soul ever turns from sin unto God, and exercises faith in the Saviour, until it is regenerated, while turning from sin unto God certainly follows regeneration, then if regeneration is the sole and exclusive act of the Holy Spirit, converts can only be made such by the Holy Spirit.

Some, however, deny that regeneration *is* the sole and exclusive act of the Holy Spirit. They reject the doctrine that the natural state of man since the fall is one of total spiritual death, and consequently they maintain that the influence by which men are regenerated is a mere suasion. These persons contend that the whole work of the Spirit in our regeneration consists in His exerting an influence on our minds by the presentation of truth and motives. Regeneration being thus affected by moral suasion—by the moral power of the truth in the hands of the Spirit, the truth co-operates with the Spirit in the regenerating act, as also does the soul which yields to the influence of this moral power.

The Scriptural doctrine, however, is that raising a soul from spiritual death to spiritual life is the act of God's omnipotent agency. It is effected by the mighty power of God. So says the Apostle in Eph. i. 17-19. He tells the Ephesians that they had been quickened—regenerated—new created by the very power which wrought in Christ when God raised Him from the dead. This is only one passage out of many which teach that regeneration is a change which the Holy Spirit's power alone can accomplish.

Let it not be forgotten that we are now speaking of regeneration. It is admitted that in conversion (*i. e.*, in the turning of the soul from sin unto God) and in exercising faith, which are the effects of regeneration, and imply it, the soul is active and co-operates with the Divine Spirit. Faith, we say, implies regeneration; but no man is for that reason excusable for refusing to believe in Christ until he knows that he is regenerated. To obey the gospel call (and to believe in Jesus is to obey the gospel call), is the immediate duty of all who hear that call. All who when they hear the call obey it as the jailer of Philippi did, are saved. Paul said to him, *i. e.*, the gospel call to him was, " Believe on the Lord Jesus Christ, and thou shalt be saved." Had he rejected Christ thus offered to him he would have been conscious that he did it voluntarily and deliberately. When the believer looks back upon the years of his impenitency, he mourns that he so long and so constantly rejected the blessed Saviour. He knows that he did it deliberately and freely. He knows, indeed, that the sin is now forgiven by Him whom he rejected, but that does not remove his sorrow for it and he does not forgive himself. The unrenewed in Christian lands are living in this sin, but they are conscious that they are not forced to reject Christ—that they do it of their own free will. Instead of feeling that they are not accountable in the matter, they know that they reject the Saviour as free agents, and that they are justly condemned because they love darkness rather than light.

Thus it is seen that the Holy Spirit alone can make a convert, because He alone regenerates the soul.

But, secondly, there is another way in which the affirmation can be shown to be true.

If we should say that a Christian is one who has passed from a state of spiritual death to a state of spiritual life, who has been created anew by the regenerating act of the Holy Spirit, who has undergone a transformation of nature so as to be in some degree holy, as God is holy, we should assert what is true, and yet this is not a full description of a Christian. Nor would a Christian be fully described if we should add to this that he is one, who having received spiritual life, has turned with grief and hatred of his sin unto God. When we explain what we mean by a Christian, we do indeed affirm these things of him, but we feel that our representation is incomplete unless we describe him as one who worships, loves, trusts, and obeys the Lord Jesus Christ.

Now, a convert does not differ from any other Christian except in this, that he has only been a Christian a short time, and is therefore immature. The spiritual life and the spiritual perceptions of a convert are precisely the same as to their nature as those of all Christians, and he has, as the object of his adoration and trust, the same blessed Saviour.

No one is a convert unless he has begun to see Jesus to be the chief among ten thousands, to apprehend the glory of God in the face of Jesus, to discern His divine loveliness, to rest upon Him, love Him, trust in Him, worship Him, and serve Him.

But not a soul in the universe can thus know, trust, love, and follow Jesus of itself. Only the Holy Spirit can take of the things of Christ and show them into the soul, and therefore those only can be converts who are made such by the Spirit of God.

To the natural man the Lord Jesus is as a root out of a dry ground, one in whom there is no form nor comeliness. It is as true of the

Saviour now as it was in the apostle's days, that He is disallowed indeed of men, but chosen of God and precious.* Only to those who are the subjects of the work of the Holy Spirit can these words be addressed with any meaning: "That the trial of your faith, being much more precious than of gold that perisheth, though it be tried with fire, might be found unto praise and honor and glory at the appearing of Jesus Christ: whom having not seen, ye love; in whom, though now ye see him not, yet believing, ye rejoice with joy unspeakable and full of glory." † Let it never be forgotten, then, that poor, lost, blind, perishing sinners, though richly deserving eternal punishment for their sins, and especially for the sin of rejecting Christ, can never be made true converts except by the Holy Spirit.

2. *Although none are really converts, except those whom the Holy Spirit has made such, many regard themselves as converts who have never been the subjects of the Spirit's saving work, and who are therefore self-deceived.*

---

* 1 Pet. ii. 4. † 1 Pet. i. 7.

Our Lord, in His parable of the sower, presents to us a class of hearers of the Word who, under the common operations of the Spirit, exercise a temporary faith, which, however, is *only* temporary, and who even receive the Word with joy. The faith which they exercise, and which has the appearance of being genuine, not only produces joy, but, for a while, seems to produce *other* effects of a saving belief, for they do many things, discharge their religious duties with alacrity, and even practise severe self-denial with cheerfulness. It is no matter for surprise, however, that this class of hearers fall away, for they are like the seed which had no root, of which our Saviour speaks in His parable, and which, therefore, notwithstanding that it sprung up at first with every appearance of health and vigor, was scorched as soon as the sun reached his meridian.

What is described in our Saviour's parable has always been, and is still going on, especially, perhaps, in seasons of revival. You will see many who, having attended to the presentation of the Word, are brought under conviction. They feel the power of the truth because their conscience is aroused and enlightened, and yields to the truth an irresistible assent. Their conviction terminates in a hope of acceptance, and this hope produces joy. But their outward duties which they begin to practise—their new mode of life—ere long becomes burdensome. By degrees they relax their efforts, and finally become like those who have never made any profession. The secret of their falling away is that they never had any true grace existing in their hearts. Their faith is not that which is exercised by a soul truly renewed. It is not founded on the illumination of the Holy Spirit; it is founded only on the assent of an awakened conscience. No wonder these hearers are unable to withstand the world's temptations.

The thorny-ground hearers present us with still another class of self-deceived converts. They are the apparent converts who speedily become steeped in the cares, the riches, and the pleasures of this life. The world, in some one of its forms, absorbs their whole attention and thus destroys the influence of the truth which had begun to affect their hearts, just as the thorns in our Saviour's parable sprung up with the seed, choked it, and so prevented it from bringing forth fruit.

When self-deceived converts, such as the thorny-ground and stony-ground hearers, are spoken of as falling away, or going back to the world, it is not meant that they certainly become immoral in their lives, or that they always forsake the house of God. They may continue to be steady attendants on the preaching of the Word, and they may ever be found in their places at the Lord's table. But they may properly be said to fall away if they relapse into a state of carnal security, and if during the remainder of their lives they attend to their religious duties as a matter of form, and without any relish for them. Nor is it meant that their case is necessarily hopeless. Would their pastors and the other church officers, and also all their fellow communicants, with tender solicitude, watch over them as our Lord requires all church members to watch over each other, they might yet be converted, although their case may seem discouraging in consequence of their having gone so far as to join the Church while in an unconverted state.

The danger of self-deception is not sufficiently dwelt upon by ministers of the gospel, and yet how many professors, without any intention to appear what they are not, are only Christians in name, have never experienced the new birth, and are still dead in trespasses and sins! That those who seek admission into the visible Church are in great danger of deceiving themselves, and that many already in the Church remain in delusion, and at last perish, is apparent from the alarming declarations of Christ in Matt. vii. 21–23.

Many self-deceived professors think that they have good reason to be satisfied that all is well with them on this ground, viz., that the officers of the church upon examining them at the time of their admission, judged them to be true Christians. They do not consider that those who are appointed to receive persons into the visible Church never pretend to feel certain that those whom they receive as Church members are true believers. They admit that they have no power to read the heart, and to tell what is going on within the soul of another. The truth is they are required by Christ to receive into the Church all applicants who profess to exercise faith in Jesus, whose profession is credible. They are never to be considered as passing any judgment on the validity of the evidence given by the applicant. Let no Church member then rest his assurance that he is a true Christian on the favorable opinion of his case, formed by the church office bearers at the time of his admission.

We are not to ascribe that conviction of sin and enlightenment of conscience, and temporary faith with its accompanying joy, which we often witness in spurious converts to the *mere* power of the truth. Even those exercises of soul which are not of a holy nature, much as they resemble the religious exercises of the regenerated, would never have any existence but for that influence of the Spirit usually called common grace which attends the truth wherever it is proclaimed, and which, in a greater or less measure, is granted to all who hear the word.

As long as the heart is deceitful, and Satan is

busy, and church officers are unable to read the heart, there will always be additions to the Church of unconverted persons, but these additions would be less frequent than they are were all pastors skilful and diligent in warning their hearers as to the danger of indulging false hopes, and in explaining to them the nature of true religion. Many have felt that there is often too great haste in admitting the hopefully converted to sealing ordinances. Says the late Dr. Spencer, in his "Pastor Sketches:" "Admission to the sealing ordinances of the Church, especially in times of revival, is a point of no little danger. Our ministers and churches have too often erred on this point. It seems to be too often forgotten that then the popular feeling tends into the Church. Fashion is that way, and sympathy that way, and all the common influences which the young are particularly likely to feel tend to urge them forward in the same direction. Far better would it be for the purity of the Church, and for the comfort and salvation of individuals, if some few months were allowed to pass before the hopefully converted were received into the communion."

As to unconverted persons who are already *communicants*, if more faithful efforts were put forth to save even *them*, such efforts would doubtless be attended with the happiest results.

The distinguished servant of Christ, from whose work the above quotation is made, was a model pastor in regard to the duty of watching over those who had already joined the Church. Speaking of certain members of his church over whom his heart yearned, and for whom he felt a deep solicitude lest they had become communicants without having been truly converted, he says : " I afterwards sought out every one of them, and alone they opened their hearts to me," and the happiest results, as we are led to infer, rewarded his faithfulness to these members.

He adds, "But it is a very difficult and laborious thing for a minister to deal with such cases. But he ought to deal with them. He will seldom labor in vain ; and while engaged in this field of duty he is engaged in the best field of study. His work then lies nearest his heart, and he cannot fail to know the human heart more accurately, and learn how to apply the powers of his mind, and the truth of God to souls ready to perish."

3. *Souls may be converted, and are in fact constantly converted, at other times than in seasons of revival.*

If by a revival we mean a great and sudden multiplication of believers — the simultaneous conversion of many persons, then, of course, it is not through revivals that the children of the covenant come into the visible Church.

But setting aside the children of believers, immense numbers come from the world into the Church at other times than in revivals. The conversion of many is spoken of in the Bible who were not brought into the Church during periods of revival, as the conversion of Zaccheus the publican; of the woman who washed the Saviour's feet with tears; of the thief crucified with our blessed Saviour; of Cornelius, the Roman centurion; of Lydia; of the Eunuch, the treasurer of the Queen of Ethiopia; of Saul of Tarsus, and his companions, Barnabas, Apollos, Timothy, Titus, Aquila and Priscilla, Epaphroditus, Onesemus and others. During the centuries that are past, and in all countries where the Church has been planted, the labors of pastors and private church members have been fruitful in the steady quiet ingathering of souls without revivals. It cannot be denied that this is one of the methods of advancing His kingdom, which the Saviour chooses to employ.

And yet some unhesitatingly proclaim that revivals are the only or almost the only means of promoting religion. This error leads many to teach, not only that it depends entirely on ourselves whether we enjoy these visitations or not — that God would at any time send them, were the desire for them sufficiently strong, but to appeal to particular passages of Scripture (as for example certain prophecies of the Old Testament) as containing promises of God to grant revivals at any season the petitioner may specify.

When a believer importunately prays that God would give His Holy Spirit, he can plead numerous express promises that such a prayer shall be heard — he is able to present to his Heavenly Father *this* reason why he should grant the request, viz., that there are plain promises in the Scriptures to bestow the Holy Spirit on all who ask for Him. And in like manner when he intercedes for the Saviour's Church, or for the world of perishing men, he can appeal to explicit assurances given in the Bible that prayer for the descent of the Spirit upon the Church of God, and upon men, shall be answered literally. But there is no promise in the Bible that prayer for the descent of the Holy Spirit on a particular church at a particular time shall meet with a literal answer. It is admitted that it is freely permitted us to offer such a request if we confide in the Saviour's love for us, and for His Church, and in His willingness to do what will be best for His cause. But we can point to no express promise that such prayer will inevitably secure the help of the Holy Spirit at the time, and in the way we specify. For a revival preacher therefore to say to a church: "You will certainly have an outpouring of the Holy Spirit at the expiration of ten days or a fortnight from now, if you will but pray for it," is presumptuous. And yet we knew a revival preacher to say this, and to warn the people not to come hastily to a conclusion adverse to his prediction, but to wait till ten days or two weeks had expired, and they would certainly see his prediction fulfilled. And sometimes revival preachers, at the beginning of the protracted meetings about to be held, publicly and ostentatiously thank God for the revival which *they are certain* He will send before the series of meetings is concluded. The only proper object of faith is some revelation of God, but it is nowhere revealed that it is God's purpose to give a particular church a revival at a time the petitioner may fix upon, provided that petitioner's prayer is sincere and oft repeated.

Errors of this kind men naturally fall into who limit the Holy One of Israel *to* revivals, and think that this is the only way in which the Saviour's kingdom can be built up. Souls are constantly converted at other times than in seasons of revival.

It is the happiness of almost every one to know faithful pastors whose churches, using only the ordinary means of grace, have prospered and increased by the constant addition of converts. A pastor speaking lately of the events of his thirty years' pastorate, said: "Revivals, technically so called, have not marked our history, but we have had long periods of ingathering, without greatly multiplying our services, and without painful reaction." The church of this servant of God, though not visited by revivals, has on three different occasions been able to give away members and families to form separate organizations, and these are now three flourishing churches.

We, of course, rejoice to acknowledge what is so evident, that it is God's design that the work of redemption should be carried on in part by means of revivals. Though each particular church would, on the whole, prosper more by a regular normal increase than by violent alternations, yet when we consider the masses, the immense fields white already to harvest, and when we consider the certainty that there are countless multitudes who will continue to be neglected, and who will never have salvation unless they have it quickly, we feel that revivals in our world, powerful works of grace, are absolutely necessary. We have only intended to remind the reader, that since there are often accessions to the Church when there are no revivals, in speaking of the great needs of converts in this little book, and in endeavoring to awaken a deeper interest in them, we do not have exclusive reference to those who are added to the Church in revival times. But we now add that,

4. *Countless numbers of converts have been in times past, and will be in future times the fruits of revivals.*

Although not all who lived in the Apostle's days were converted in seasons of remarkable awakenings, yet we know that three thousand of Peter's hearers were on the day of Pentecost thus gathered in. In the primitive age, and in what we call the reformation period, there was a succession of glorious revivals, and doubtless it was in these seasons that the principal part of believers then in the world had been converted.

There have been times when it could have been said with truth of the larger portion of church members in many sections of our own country, that they had been brought into the

Saviour's kingdom during the progress of revivals. There are yet to be many such visitations before the second appearing of our blessed Lord. This can be doubted by no one. Remote, indeed, must be the establishment of our dear Lord's kingdom on the ruins of Satan's kingdom, unless our poor world is to be favored with numerous and powerful effusions of the Spirit, resulting in many precious harvests of souls. We should desire such precious harvests for all classes, not excluding the depraved multitude—the lowest and the vilest. "Could we unroof the dense portions of our great cities, and look into the dens of drink and debauchery, we should behold undeniable signs of wounded spirits, without hope, without God. The gospel was made for such, and has saved such. Amidst the reiterated and increasing prayers which go up for the outpouring of the Spirit, surely there ought to be importunate supplication for influences to penetrate these lowest strata. Awakening is incomplete unless it go deeper, far deeper down than our well-dressed throngs. We also crave it for the abject and the abandoned. The blind and the vicious, from whose ranks the levies are made for riots and prisons, will not flock to the preached word until some fresh and irresistible influence, affecting the whole population, find its way to the very scenes of their nocturnal orgies. We can think of nothing more likely to compel the attention of blasphemous, base, and even violent men and women, than a mighty tide of revival, pressing its repeated waves into their miserable homes and hearts. Our blessed Lord has taught us that these not only need the truth, but are accessible to its power. "Jesus saith unto them, Verily I say unto you, That the publicans and the harlots go into the kingdom of God before you."

The time is coming when, if the Church is to overspread the earth, there will be far more glorious revivals than have yet been witnessed, and she will be guilty of unspeakable folly unless she endeavors to be prepared for these ingatherings; and in no way can she be better prepared for them than by using every means in her power to qualify herself for the work of training the converts who are to be the fruits of the revivals which are to be sent, and of building them up in the faith. And since powerful outpourings of the Spirit will be as much needed in future times as in times gone by, it is a matter of the utmost importance that all her members avoid every act and every sinful neglect which may prove a hindrance to such effusions.

5. *The exercises of soul previously to conversion, and also subsequently to this great change, differ in different converts.*

Conviction of sin is indeed essentially the same in all who are the subjects of it. All under conviction feel that they deserve, and are exposed to, eternal death, because of their want of conformity to God's law. They also feel that their sinfulness is pollution and renders them morally offensive, the objects of disapprobation and abhorrence. In addition to this, they see and feel that they are helpless, in that they cannot make any atonement for their guilt, nor deliver themselves from the dominion which sin has over them. All true converts had this sense of sin, of ill desert, of inward pollution, and of helplessness previously to their passing from death to life. They have it, indeed, afterward and during their whole Christian course, but *then*, i. e., after they have actually become Christians, it is accompanied with an apprehension of God's mercy, through Jesus Christ, with a sorrow which is godly and holy, and with filial feelings.

But although conviction of sin is essentially the same in all souls awakened, but not yet converted, there is discovered also the greatest diversity; the effects of such conviction " being modified by the temperament, the knowledge, the circumstances, and concomitant exercises of those who experience it. A sentence of death if passed upon a hundred men would probably affect no two alike. The mind of one might fasten particularly on the turpitude of his crime; that of another upon the disgrace which he had incurred; that of a third on the sufferings of his friends on his account; that of a fourth upon the horrors of death, or upon the fearfulness of appearing before God. All these and many other views in endless combination might operate with different degrees of force on each, and the result be still further modified by their physical and moral temperament, their knowledge and previous history. The endless diversity, therefore, in the experience of men when convinced of sin, is what might be expected."

Converts also differ among themselves as to their experience immediately after coming to Christ, and that notwithstanding that the exercises of piety are always essentially the same. "There are doubtless great diversities in the appearances of the motions and actings of piety in its incipient stages. Some at the time of their new birth are brought at once into the clear light of day. They are as if introduced into a new world. The sun of righteousness has risen upon them without an intervening cloud. Their perception of divine things is so new, and so clear that they feel persuaded that they can convince others and cause them to see and feel as they do. Such persons can no more doubt of their conversion than of their existence." On the other hand the new exercises of the religious life of others are very faint, and yet these latter may eventually far exceed in piety and excellence of character those who commenced their Christian life with more lively religious views and feelings. There is, however, no good reason why those converts whose souls are richly blessed in the very beginning of their Christian course, should afterward lose the benefit of their sweet early experiences, if they persevere from the first, in the earnest and diligent use of the means of grace.

The following is an account of the remarkable early religious exercises of the great and good Dr. Archibald Alexander, whose progress in piety was, it cannot be doubted, without any interruption to the very close of his long and useful life: "I read all the religious narratives I could procure, and labored much to put myself into the state in which others described themselves to have been before enjoying hope. But all these efforts and desires proved abortive, and I began to see much more of the wickedness of my own heart than ever before. I was distressed and discouraged, and convinced that I had placed too much dependence on mere means, and on my own efforts. I therefore determined to give myself incessantly to prayer until I found mercy, or perished in the pursuit.

"This resolution was formed on a Sunday evening. The next morning I took my Bible and walked several miles into the dense wood of the Bushy Hills, which were then wholly uncultivated. Finding a place that pleased me, at the foot of a projecting rock, in a dark valley, I began, with great earnestness, the course which I had prescribed to myself. I prayed, and then read in the Bible, prayed and read, prayed and read, until my strength was exhausted; for I had taken no nourishment that day. But the more I strove the harder my heart became, and the more barren was my mind of every serious or tender feeling. I tasted then some of the bitterness of despair. It seemed to be my last resource, and now this had utterly failed. I was about to desist from the endeavor, when the thought occurred to me, that though I was helpless, and my case was nearly desperate, yet it would be well to cry to God to help me in this extremity. I knelt upon the ground and had poured out perhaps a single petition, or rather broken cry for help, when, in a moment, I had such a view of a crucified Saviour, as is without a parallel in my experience. The whole plan of grace appeared as plain as day. I was persuaded that God was willing to accept me, just as I was, and convinced that I had never before understood the freeness of salvation, but had always been striving to bring some price in my hand, or to prepare myself for receiving Christ. Now I discovered that I could receive Him in all his offices at that very moment, which I was sure at the time I did. I felt truly a joy which was unspeakable and full of glory. How long this delightful frame continued I cannot tell. But when my affections had a little subsided, I opened my Bible and alighted on the eighteenth and nineteenth chapters of John. The sacred page appeared to be illuminated; the truths were new, as if I had never read them before; and I thought it would be always thus. Having often thought of engaging in a written covenant with God, but having never before found a freedom to do so, I now felt no hesitation, and, having writing materials in my pocket, I sat down and penned it exactly from my feelings, and solemnly signed it as in the presence of God.

"I expected now to feel uniformly different from what had preceded, and to be always in lively emotion, thinking my troubles all at an end. As I had been much distressed by discovering the sins of my heart, and as I had read in Scripture that faith works purification, I resolved to make this the test. At the time, indeed, I had no doubt as to the sincerity of my faith; and in the paper of self-dedication above mentioned, I expressed the assurance that if I had never before received Christ, I did then and there receive Him. For several days my mind was serene. But before a week had elapsed, darkness began to gather over me again. Inbred corruption began to stir. In a word, I fell back into the same state of darkness and conflict as before."

This state of mind continued for some time, even after he had made a profession of his faith. But, on looking back in after life, he expresses his belief that the exercises given above were genuine, and that the period of darkness that followed those exercises, did not prove that he had not been regenerated.

CHAPTER II.

INDUCEMENTS WHICH SHOULD STIMULATE THE PEOPLE OF GOD TO ENGAGE IN THE WORK OF HELPING CONVERTS.

PERHAPS you have a dear friend who was until lately in bondage to sin and Satan, but who, in answer to your fervent and importunate prayers in his behalf, offered for many years, is now a true disciple of Jesus. What are your feelings when you think of this friend for whose salvation you so earnestly and perseveringly prayed? What are the intense desires of your soul with reference to him? Are they not that he should steadily grow in the divine life, and become stronger and stronger to resist evil and to practise all Christian excellencies? And in the efforts which you earnestly make to be of service to him, and to help him, are not those efforts called forth by your knowledge that he is, as yet, weak as a

Christian, and has many and exceedingly great spiritual wants needing attention? Do you not feel that it is enough to induce you to exert yourself in his behalf, that he has dangers and trials always incident to spiritual infancy, and is as yet without that experience and those attainments which the advanced Christian possesses? Now the graces of all converts are in like manner as yet untried, and less developed than those of older believers, and on this account they all have wants, the neglect of which must render their condition perilous. And this is a sufficient reason, even should no others be mentioned, why Christians who have for years been followers of the Saviour, should strive to be useful to the Church's converts, should watch over, cherish, encourage, warn, and instruct them. There are, however, other inducements of equal weight, which are, perhaps, less likely to be considered.

1. *The Saviour has expressly committed them to your care.*

He has committed them to your care by calling them His brethren. For doubtless, among others our blessed Lord will have them in His mind, when at the last day He will say to those on His right hand—"Inasmuch as ye have done it unto one of the least of these my brethren, ye have done it unto me." He has committed them to your care by telling you also what He has done for them. He tells you that He loved them before the world began. He tells you that this love constrained Him to die for them. He tells you that He has forgiven all their sins, accepted them, and bestowed upon them a title to everlasting life. That He will tenderly watch over them, chastising them when they wander away from Him, and preserving them from falling from grace. That He will always intercede for them, and will at last receive them unto Himself, where they will be where He is, and forever behold His glory. And then they will be perfect, full of sweetness, purity, and every excellence. Christ has committed them to your care also, by uniting them to you in the closest of bonds, for as He has made you members of His body, so He has made them. As the branch is one with the vine so are they, in common with you, one with Christ. It is as true of them that they are united to Christ by the Holy Spirit's indwelling, as it is of you. The Spiritual life which dwells in Christ, abides in you no more truly than it does in them.

Moreover, when we consider certain commands which Christ has given us, we cannot but feel that He has committed converts to our care. He commands us to deny ourselves for the good of our brethren, to bear their burdens, to place no stumbling-block in their way, to rejoice with them in their seasons of joy, and to weep with them in their times of sorrow. He commands us further to be kindly affectioned to our brethren, to distribute to their necessities, to warn and admonish them, to walk circumspectly before them, to give freely to them of the things which we have freely received, to visit them, to pray for them, to avoid everything whereby they may stumble, or be offended, or be made weak, and to be especially anxious to do them good because they are of the household of faith. In laying these commands upon us, our Saviour enjoins it upon us to do good to converts, for all converts are our brethren.

"Hereby perceive we the love of God," says the apostle, "because He laid down His life for us: and we ought to lay down our lives for the brethren. But whoso hath this world's good, and seeth his brother have need, and shutteth up his bowels of compassion from him, how dwelleth the love of God in him?" If we prove that we have not the love of God in us when, possessing this world's goods, we shut up our bowels of compassion from a fellow Christian in want of temporal supplies, how much stronger proof do we furnish of being destitute of the love of God when we refuse to minister to the spiritual wants of those of our fellow disciples whom our Saviour calls His lambs.

2. *You have the example of the apostles in this thing, and of the Church's early laborers.*

There are those who are willing to labor to bring unconverted souls into the kingdom of Christ, but who do not care about having anything more to do with them afterward. It was not so with the great apostle. The temptations to which his converts were exposed, the dangers which surrounded them, their weakness of faith and want of stability, as also their afflictions and persecutions, deeply affected him and filled him with anxiety. To hear of their attainments in knowledge and holiness, or of any manifestation on their part of love for the brethren, or of docility in receiving his teachings, or of zeal for the Master's cause, awakened within him the sincerest joy. He addressed none of his letters to unconverted men. Abundant and successful as were his labors for *their* salvation, it was to immature and inexperienced believers—to converts, that most of his letters were addressed. For the several churches of Corinth, Galatia, Philippi, etc., were, at the time of his composing his epistles for them, in the infancy of their existence. Thus we see the pains which the great apostle took to instruct those who had but just begun the Christian life. Examine his letters and see the fulness, the variety, the wisdom, and preciousness of his instructions.

Of what solid food would Paul's converts have been deprived had he not written these letters to them?

We see the strength and tenderness of Paul's love for his converts by the manner in which he speaks of them. He calls them his brethren, his dearly beloved, his joy and crown. The deep interest which he continually felt in them may also be seen in what is said of his labors for them in the Acts of the Apostles. He did not forget those whom he had been instrumental in converting, but revisited them. We are told that the hearts of Paul and Barnabas yearned over those who, under their preaching, had been converted in Antioch, Lystra, and Iconium, and they had left them but a short time before they returned to them for the purpose of building them up, strengthening their faith, comforting them, and warning them of what they had to expect. The words are, "They returned again to Lystra, and to Iconium, and Antioch, confirming the souls of the disciples, and exhorting them to continue in the faith, and that we must through much tribulation enter into the kingdom of God."

The Antioch here mentioned was the one in the province of Pisidia, in Asia Minor. At the other Antioch, which was the capital of Syria, and where the disciples were first called

Christians, some of the brethren had been very successful in preaching the gospel after they had fled to the place from Jerusalem when the persecution began there, against the Church. When the news of these conversions came to the Church which was in Jerusalem they sent Barnabas to visit the new believers of Antioch. " Who, when he came, and had seen the grace of God, was glad, and exhorted them all, that with purpose of heart they would cleave unto the Lord." Thus it was that the new converts were remembered. Thus it was that they were visited and encouraged.

We also should remember the immense benefit which converts are capable of receiving from labors put forth for their good, and we should imitate the example of Christ's servants who lived in apostolic times. In all ages and times, young disciples have peculiar trials and dangers and difficulties, and piety must always be progressive in its nature. It is therefore the duty of Christ's people at the present day, as well as in former times, to confirm the souls of those whose Christian life has but just commenced.

3. *Almost all converts are sadly neglected.*

Should one on whom all eyes are fastened, a man of great ability and influence, and occupying a distinguished position in the counsels of the nation, become a Christian, and should it everywhere be known that he has professed to be a disciple of Christ, not a few of the people of God would earnestly pray that he might be steadfast. His growth in Christian excellence would be intensely desired. He would be watched, and any indication of his progress in goodness, in zeal for God's glory, in solicitude for the Church's advancement, and for the spiritual welfare of men would be hailed with joy. Many Christians would intercede for him that he might be strengthened to resist temptations to worldliness, and might be a helper to Zion's laborers, and of great service to the Redeemer's cause. All this would be natural. It would be strange indeed if God's people should not have their attention especially called to a convert of this description, one filling a conspicuous position, and pre-eminent for his gifts and his influence.

There have been instances in which a powerful ruler of some heathen people—one having his mind full of heathen prejudices against the Christian religion has become a convert to the faith, and has apparently become a humble Christian; and when such an event has occurred, thanksgiving and praise have ascended from the hearts of a multitude of believers. They have felt a deep interest in his spiritual condition. Now it is freely admitted that such converts are the objects of the love of the blessed Saviour, and that the angels of Heaven rejoice over their repentance. But does the blessed Redeemer, and do the angels make that difference which we make, between the conversion of such and the conversion of persons of more obscure position? When any immortal soul becomes, as we have reason to believe, an heir of glory, the event should deeply affect us. The most lively interest should be felt in every newly regenerated soul, whatever his station in life.

And yet souls are constantly delivered from the power of darkness, and translated into the kingdom of God's dear Son, in whom scarcely any interest is taken, and for whose spiritual good such little effort is put forth, that we may justly speak of them as neglected converts. We fear it is true of almost all who become the disciples of Jesus, that they have no one to begin immediately to care for their spiritual progress. Seeing then that so few in the Church of Christ are faithful to the new disciples who have entered her fold, let them have the benefit of your prayers, and of whatever other efforts you can make to advance them in the blessed life which they have begun to live. Do not imitate those who expend all their interest and efforts on converts of conspicuous station, while they feel far less concern for the numerous converts of inferior position and influence.

4. *You should feel the deepest interest in all those recently born from above, when you consider that they are living in a world in which all their relations of a spiritual nature are new to them.*

We know the relation of hostility which all converts alike sustained, until within a short time, to the law of God, to God Himself, to the blessed Jesus, and to Christ's Church and people; and the friendly terms on which they all stood to the world, and to the entire kingdom which is opposed to the Saviour's kingdom. Until recently they were all under God's displeasure (for they that are in the flesh cannot please God), and were also God's enemies. They every day rejected Christ. Not being for Him, they were against Him. They always resisted the Holy Spirit. The blessed Spirit was neither their Teacher, Comforter, nor Sanctifier. They were Satan's subjects, were members of that empire which is at war with the Church, and so they were the Church's enemies. We who now recognize them as our brethren are compelled to acknowledge that until recently this was their attitude to holy persons and things, just as once it was ours. Only a short time has passed since all these relations on their part to the spiritual world have changed. It is a new thing to them to be accounted the children of God. To be free from the unchallenged and unceasing dominion of sin, to be free from the law's dreadful curse, to be heirs of glory, possessed of a title to eternal life, to be disenthralled from Satan's bondage, to be members of Christ, and of His blood-bought Church, to be the loving and beloved brethren of all Christians, all this is new to them. And is there nothing in all this which is fitted to awaken your deepest interest in the Church's converts—in all her converts?

A change having taken place in their relation to God and to His law, they have undergone a change in their inward character. Up to a very late period of their history they were in character completely separated from God and from heaven's holy inhabitants, but, during the few days, or weeks, or months in which they have been believers in Jesus, God, the angels, and all perfectly holy beings have been able to look upon their inward character with the love of complacency. Being now in some degree holy they have new, and fresh, and joyful views of God, of Christ, of the gospel, and of the life to come, and their hearts are the home of all gracious affections.

5. *Of some converts it may be said with truth that the work of endeavoring to benefit them is pleasant in itself, and the probability of success is most encouraging.*

It is pleasant in the case of some, because

when you approach them they meet you without any restraint of manner, with a delightful whole-heartedness, and, at the moment when they are in all the freshness of their first love. They are living in a world which is new to them. They enjoy a sweet rest of soul. The Lord is dealing tenderly with them. They have not, as yet, found anything irksome or burdensome in religious duties. They meet you promptly and affectionately, and your heart warms toward them, and the last thing you think of is that efforts to warn, or encourage, or guide them, are going to be painful. Your work is not only pleasant, but it is likely to be successful, provided you are judicious, cautious, and persevering. For you will meet with few of those difficulties which are very often encountered by the faithful minister, or private church member who seeks to help older professors of religion. For when some among *them* are conversed with, it is found that they are depressed and weakened by discouraging remembrances of broken resolutions and past failures. The convert knows nothing of this. He is hopeful, though this may, in part, be owing to his ignorance of the trials and dangers which are before him. But it is by no means necessary that he should sink under these when called to contend with them. If he begins his Christian life as he ought to begin it, that of itself will greatly promote his real progress. Expect success then in your endeavors to be of service to Christ's young disciples, and you will not be disappointed.

6. *Many converts had but little religious instruction in early life.*

The superior knowledge of the Scriptures, which some Christians possess, is due, in almost all cases, to the fact that they were carefully taught the truth of God in childhood and youth. In consequence of having been thus early instructed, they knew much about the Bible even before they were regenerated. They had clear views of the plan of salvation, of the nature of Christ's work, and of the nature and office of the Holy Spirit. They had some understanding of the manner in which we are made partakers of the redemption purchased by Christ. They comprehended very much of the system of truth as it is contained in the Word of God. This knowledge, however, as long as it was only speculative, could not save them, but, as soon as they were regenerated, they immediately had a spiritual perception of the divine beauty and glory of the truth, already lodged in their minds, founded on the Holy Spirit's illumination, and thus the truth began to bring forth the fruits of holiness in their lives. They also began to thirst for further divine knowledge, and to make earnest efforts to attain it. In this manner, as was said, is to be explained the superior knowledge of the truth which some Christians possess. *They were carefully instructed in early life.*

But it may be that many converts, who are within the reach of your influence, had been, up to the time of their regeneration, without such instruction. Since they, also, are now the subjects of God's grace, and are enlightened by the Holy Spirit, it is to be supposed, indeed, that they, likewise, will have a sincere desire for further knowledge of the things which God has revealed, but, in consequence of their lack of early instruction, you find them exceedingly ignorant. You would have to say, it may be, of many of them, what Baxter wrote concerning some who attended upon his ministry, who had not been taught the system of truth when they were young. He says: "I am daily forced to admit how lamentably ignorant many of our people are that have seemed diligent hearers of me these ten or twelve years, while I spoke as plainly as I was able to speak. Some know not that each person in the Trinity is God; nor that Christ is God and man; nor that He took His human nature into heaven; nor many the like necessary principles of our faith." Seeing, then, there are many converts of this description, who need to have their sad want of early religious instruction made up to them, what a motive you have to cultivate the habit of striving to do good to all believers within your reach, who are young in the Christian life.

7. *Many suffer great loss in consequence of their slowness to disclose their conflicts and difficulties.*

Many converts have but a trembling hope of their own acceptance. Their faith and hope are not sufficiently strong to exclude painful anxieties about their spiritual state. Others enjoy a comfortable hope that their salvation is really begun, who have perplexities which they are not able to dismiss from their minds about the teachings of the Bible concerning certain doctrines. Others are sorely tried by doubts as to how they should act in the peculiar circumstances in which they are placed. And still others often find it difficult to resist the temptation to indulge in practices lawful in themselves, but which in their case would be sinful, the lawfulness of such practices not being to *their* minds clear. Now it is of the utmost importance that young believers, who have such inward difficulties and struggles, should not keep them locked up in their own bosoms, but should disclose them. It is possible for them to be aided by the counsels and instructions of their more experienced brethren. In order, however, that they may be encouraged to disclose their trials, they must see a readiness in their fellow church-members to help them. They should be urged, in a spirit of love, to make their conflicts known. Their reluctance to speak of their inward troubles might be overcome by a little solicitation, provided you use the tact which is necessary for the right performance of so delicate a duty, for it cannot be denied that the attempt to benefit men by such approaches to them is a delicate one. "The reserve which most people feel in reference to laying bare their inmost thoughts, the painful burden borne in silence often so long, the shrinking from observation, the Nicodemus-like approach of many souls to Christ for light, ought to instruct us to walk softly here." Still, you need not be deterred from the attempt to win the confidence even of the most sensitive, if you are actuated by the sincerest love for them, and if God gives you wisdom, which he will give you, in answer to prayer. Let it be your habit, then, to give attention to the needs of converts, for you may then frequently enjoy opportunities of encouraging them to disclose their doubts and struggles of mind instead of concealing them to their own injury.

Should you succeed in winning their confidence, and should you really be helpful to them, you yourself will receive benefit. You will have the comfort of knowing that you have done good to some, who, but for you, would probably have been entirely neglected. The Saviour will bestow upon you the reward which He reserves for those who care for, and feed —"the little ones"—the lambs of His flock, for He numbers converts among the little ones who believe on Him. You will learn much concerning the forbearance, mercy, patience, and compassion of Christ for those whom He came to seek and to save. These precious words will often be present to your mind: "He shall feed His flock like a shepherd; He shall gather the lambs with His arm, and carry them in His bosom, and shall gently lead those that are with young." Moreover, the very truths with which you seek to enlighten and strengthen the untaught and inexperienced young Christian will be promotive of your own spiritual good. They will come home to your own heart with power.

8. *One reason why so many professing Christians imbibe hurtful errors is that so little attention was paid to them when they were converts.*

There is no denying the fact that many who were hopefully converted fail to abide steadfastly in the truth. They may not speedily, after professing Christ, forsake the truths they had engaged and expected always to revere and obey, but the time arrives when important doctrines, after becoming gradually less esteemed, are finally given up, while erroneous views are embraced and zealously advocated. This might have been prevented had they been from the beginning really under the Church's care—had they been faithfully warned, instructed, guarded, counselled, and prayed for. But while the Church neglects her converts, Satan is not inactive. "Nor can any human faculty perceive the precise mode in which falsehood will be presented by a wily foe. Sometimes it is the vehicle which is attractive. It may, for example, be elegant style, it may be romance, it may be closely-knit argumentation, it may be popular eloquence. The union of several such fascinations may invite the youth to taste the poisonous clusters, and acquire a fondness for doubts and cavils. The name and fame of some great heretical preacher summons numbers of half-instructed people who admire, and acquiesce, and go again, not knowing that the new doctrines which they drink in will presently unsettle the religious belief of their childhood. Among the multitude of books, public journals, orations, lectures, poems, and common talk, in which we live, there are every day some which propose unscriptural, and even anti-Christian opinions. There are many who read abundance of books, but among them so little of Christian theology that they do not recognize the erroneous sentiments of unsound systems, if offered to them with prettiness of diction, pretension to philosophy, cant phrases, and the rounded voice of a popular lecturer. These false teachings often begin far away from the point at which they really aim."

Let the convert be warned in time. Let him be earnestly admonished. Let him be exhorted to continue in the faith—to hold fast his profession. Let him be cautioned against falling into the mistake of supposing that when one is truly converted, any great deception in reference to spiritual things is henceforth impossible. Let him be reminded of the frequent warnings against this very peril, addressed by Christ and His apostles even to true disciples, warnings full of meaning and power: "Take heed lest any man deceive you." "Be not deceived." "Let him that thinketh he standeth take heed lest he fall." "Let no man deceive you with vain words." "If there come any unto you, and bring not this doctrine, receive him not into your house, neither bid him God speed: for he that biddeth him God speed, is partaker of his evil deeds." Let him be taught "that the new convert whose appetite often surpasses his power of discernment, is singularly liable to be duped by error," and that salutary fear of this folly is often the means of preventing it.

9. *Many converts might be saved from wandering from the fold, and from long-continued decline, were they not so sadly neglected.*

A regenerated person may begin to grow in grace from the very start, and he may make no mean attainments, and yet he may not continue to advance long. He may never have thoroughly learned that, although God works in the believer to will and to do, yet the believer is, with fear and trembling, to work out his own salvation. Or, if at first alive to the necessity of diligence, his conviction of its necessity may gradually be blunted, and less and less realized, in consequence of his increasing attachment to the world.

Many of God's people begin to decline even in the early part of their Christian course, and, as a consequence of this, live and die without making those attainments in holiness, which it is in the power of all to make who are constantly watchful, and who are active, energetic, and unwearied in using the means of grace. The following, which we quote from Dr. Alexander's work, " Thoughts on Religious Experience," well describes the downward course of many believers, who, at first, give promise of uninterrupted progress :

" The young convert's love to the Saviour, and to the saints, is fresh and fervent, and his religious zeal, though not well regulated by knowledge, is ardent. He often puts older disciples to the blush by the warmth of his affections, and his alacrity in the service of his Redeemer. This is, indeed, the season of his first love, which began to flow in the day of his espousals; and though, occasionally, dark clouds intercept his views, these are soon forgotten, when the clear sunshine breaks forth to cheer him on his way. During this period he delights in social exercises, especially in communion with those of his own age, and in prayer, and in praise and in spiritual conversation. His heart is lifted up to heaven, and he longs for the time when he may join the songs of the upper temple. But ere long the scene changes. Gradually the glow of fervent affections subsides. Worldly pursuits, even the most lawful and necessary, steal away the heart; and various perplexing entanglements beset the inexperienced traveller. He begins to see that there were many things faulty in his early course. He blames his own weakness or enthusiasm; and in avoiding one extreme he easily falls into the opposite, to which human nature has a strong bias. He enters into more intercourse with the world, and, of course, imbibes insensibly some portion of its spirit. This has a deadening effect on his religious feelings; and his devotions are less fervent and less punctual; and far more interrupted with vain, wondering thoughts, than before; and he is apt to fall into a hasty or formal attendance on the daily duties of the closet; and a little matter will sometimes lead him to neglect these precious seasons of grace. A strange forgetfulness of the presence of God, and of his accountableness for every thought, word, and action seizes upon him. Close self-examination becomes painful, and when attempted, is unsuccessful. New evils begin to appear springing up in the heart. The imagination, before he is aware, is filled with sensual imagery, which affording carnal pleasure, the train of his thoughts is with difficulty changed. Envy, undue indulgence of the appetites, love of riches, fondness for dress and show, the love of ease, aversion to spiritual duties, with numerous similar and nameless evils, are now bred in the heart, and come forth to annoy and retard the Christian in his course. His pride makes him unwilling to open his ear to friendly and fraternal reproof; such words fall heavily on him, and wound his morbid sensibility, so that a conflict takes place between a sense of duty and unmortified pride. If, in this conflict, pride should gain the victory, alas, how much sin follows in its train—resentment toward a kind brother, hypocrisy in concealing the real dictates of conscience, and a neglect of all efforts at improvement. The person thus circumstanced, is instinctively led to endeavor to persuade himself that he has done right. Still, however, the language of his better part is that of self-condemnation. But he hushes it up, and assumes an air of innocence and boldness, and thus the Spirit is grieved. Who can describe the train of evils which ensue, on one defeat of this kind? The mind becomes dark and desolate; communion with God is interrupted, and a course of backsliding commences, which sometimes goes on for years, and then the wanderer is not arrested and brought back without severe chastisement." Cases of spiritual declension are so common that some have thought there is no way of avoiding the evil. This is going too far, but certainly the danger of declining and even of backsliding is very great, and the greatest pains should be taken to put the new disciple on his guard. Use every means, therefore, to save the convert from so terrible an evil. Fix one thought deeply in his mind : that there is no standing still—that to fail in making progress, is to go backward.

10. *You may be the means of the conversion of self-deceived converts.*

Our Saviour teaches us, in His parable of the sower, that many hear the word with attention, and even feel the power of the truth delivered. It makes an impression on them. They are not wayside hearers. They exercise a certain kind of faith. Their faith, however, is not that which saves, it is not genuine. It differs from spiritual discernment. It does not perceive the inherent beauty, sweetness, and glory of the truth. It is founded on the power of conscience, and is, therefore, capable of producing temporary obedience, and emboldens those who have it, to connect themselves with the Church, but it does not work by love, purify the heart, and overcome the world. Such persons must perish forever, as truly as the hardened and insensible, unless they are changed, and have eyes given them from above, to behold the divine glory and loveliness of Jesus, and unless they truly come to Him, look to Him, flee to Him, and rest upon Him alone for their salvation. It is just as great and blessed a thing to save such self-deceived converts, as it is to save those who make no pretension to religion. But, if you are in the habit of exerting yourself to benefit the new disciples within your reach, it may so happen that, without your knowing or designing it, you will be the means of saving such apparent converts. They may be enlightened to see, they may be brought to feel that the words of instruction, or encouragement or exhortation with which you address them, are not applicable to them, and they, seeing and feeling this, your words may alarm and awaken them. And, while they are anxious not to be again deceived, the work wrought in them may be thorough, and their repentance may be one not to be repented of. How many self-deceived professors might be enlightened to see their true condition, and be saved, did all church members faithfully fulfil their engagement to watch over each other, and to seek each other's spiritual well-being.

11. *If you are instrumental in promoting the spiritual good of converts, you will be the means of promoting the prosperity of the whole Church.*

Is it through the conversion of souls unto Jesus that the Church increases in life and power? Yes, but not in that way alone. She also advances and prospers by the growth in holiness of those whose salvation is already begun, of those who are already within her pale, and belong to her. This is one reason why the increasing spirituality of a single believer always filled the great apostle with joy. The spiritual prosperity of any disciple, for whose welfare he labored, filled him with exultation, not only because of his love for that disciple, but because he knew that thereby the entire Church received an accession of strength. He knew that the Church, like the human body, is one organic whole, and that as a consequence of this the religious advancement of the humblest believer tends to the symmetry and perfection of the entire Church. Think of this truth with comfort, whenever you hope that you have been instrumental in helping a fellow Christian —yes, a convert, whose spiritual necessities appealed to your Christian love for assistance. As no Christian can grow in grace without thereby adding in some little degree to the inward strength of the kingdom of Christ on earth, while he at the same time weakens the kingdom of Satan, so, whoever aids a Christian to grow in grace, is thereby useful to the whole Church.

The inducements presented in this chapter to aid the Saviour's converts should surely have weight with all who attentively consider them. Those who, tenderly alive to their condition and needs, have persevered in efforts to do them good, have been among Christ's most useful servants. An eminently holy and successful minister of the gospel in giving some account of the zeal and activity of a church member, says of him: "It pleased a gracious God, about the year ——, to revive religion with extraordinary power in all the country around where he lived. It was what he had prayed for night and day, but scarcely hoped to see, for he had never before witnessed what is called a revival. Almost his whole time was now spent in conversing with the new converts.

He would labor with them in the most earnest and affectionate manner, and would bring to them suitable books, for he was much conversant with the most spiritual and experimental authors, and many young disciples were deeply indebted to his faithful labors."

That you, reader, may be prepared to engage in so blessed a work, keep your own soul in a state of nearness to God and of spiritual prosperity. Speak often to your fellow Christians about the needs of converts. Learn all you can from a survey of your own earliest experiences about their dangers and wants.

CHAPTER III.

SOME OF THE DOCTRINAL TRUTHS WHICH THE CONVERT SHOULD BE ASSISTED TO APPREHEND CLEARLY, IN ORDER THAT HE MAY HAVE A HEALTHY RELIGIOUS EXPERIENCE, AND ALSO GROW IN GRACE.

WE cannot take the place of God in doing good to converts. We cannot exert that influence upon them which it belongs to the Holy Spirit alone to exert—a supernatural influence. The Spirit of God is able to dwell within their hearts, controlling and guiding, by His divine power, their inward exercises and outward conduct, until He brings them at last to the purity and blessedness of heaven. We cannot thus work within them. Neither are we able to do for converts what they must do for themselves. They are not to learn and practise Christ's commands by proxy, nor are they in this manner to use the means of grace, but each one is for himself to work out his salvation, and glorify, serve, and obey the Lord Jesus. It is only as instruments in the hands of God that we can do converts good, and the question is, How can we instrumentally benefit them? Undoubtedly by bringing them, by our instructions and in every other way in our power, to know and act upon those truths which God has commanded them to receive. Some of these truths which should be taught them we now proceed to state.

1. *It is important that the young convert should be taught that the feeling or experience of conviction of sin is not confined to the awakened sinner, but that it is an experience which characterizes every believer.*

The true believer views the character of God with complacency, loves Him, and has hope in His mercy; but these gracious affections which spring up in every new-born soul do not drive away all conviction of sin. The Christian who has begun to love, trust, and serve Jesus, still retains that part of conviction at least, which consists in a sense of sin or inward pollution. This feeling he retains after all his agitation and distress, and fear of God's wrath have entirely passed away. His sense of sin deepens and increases as he grows in grace. The Holy Spirit so enlightens him, gives him such a knowledge of himself (not all at once, but gradually), that it may sometimes seem to him that instead of making progress in holiness, he is becoming more and more sinful. This is a truer conviction of sin than that which belongs to the awakened and alarmed sinner who has not yet embraced the offer of mercy. But the conviction is not painful, because the sorrow which belongs to it is a godly sorrow. It is all the more important that the convert should receive instruction as to this, for it is extensively taught in these days that the Christian should not be in this state of mind—should not have such an experience in regard to sin, since it would show that he has not yet looked to Christ for everything, and received everything —" has not passed out of the bondage of the seventh chapter of Romans into the sweet liberty of the eighth." *

---

* "There is no difference between the experience described in Rom. viii. and that delineated in vii. 14-25. The same conflict between grace and indwelling sin is found in both chapters.

True believers, moreover, have as vivid a feeling of ill desert as they have of inward pollution. Their conscience, their whole soul tells them that they merit nothing better than the penalty of God's violated law. It tells them this, even more powerfully than it did when in a state of impenitency they were awakened from their security and brought with alarm to see their danger. It is true that being now united to Christ they may have much peace and even joy, but they can never forget that they really deserve to be banished forever from God's presence. And what their conscience

---

The person in the seventh chapter who is 'sold under sin' (vii. 14), and 'serves with the flesh the law of sin' (vii. 25), and cries, 'O wretched man, who shall deliver me' (vii. 24), and yet 'thanks God, through Jesus Christ,' for his deliverance, and 'serves with the mind the law of God' (vii. 25), belongs to that class who in the eighth chapter have been 'made free from the law of sin and death by the law of the Spirit of life' (viii. 2), and yet are exhorted 'not to live after the flesh' (viii. 12), and to 'mortify the deeds of the body' (viii. 13), who 'have received the Spirit of adoption, crying, Abba, Father' (viii. 15), and yet 'groan within themselves, waiting for the adoption, to wit, the redemption of the body' (viii. 23), and 'with patience wait for' sinless perfection and heavenly blessedness (viii. 25)."— Dr. Shedd's "Com. on Romans."

and their whole soul tells them as to this, is true as a matter of fact. Though God's children and the objects of His love, and free from condemnation, they are, in fact, deserving of condemnation and of the curse which the law has denounced against sin. And they will, as a matter of fact, be deserving of it in heaven, notwithstanding they will in heaven be perfectly holy and happy.

When a saint enters heaven he enters that blessed abode free from condemnation, *i.e.*, with his sentence to eternal death removed, and with a title to eternal life. This, indeed, he enjoyed while in the body, and abiding on earth — he enjoyed it from the moment when he began to trust in Jesus to save him. He also enters heaven perfectly holy, not because he was perfectly holy in this life (though in this life he was, *in some degree*, holy) but because he was made perfect in holiness at the moment of death. But while these two things are true of the believer when he passes into glory, it is not true of him that he passes into glory deserving any blessing whatever. He is ill deserving as he enters heaven, and will be so forever; nor will this fact ever be forgotten by him. He will never be weary of acknowledging it as he ascribes praise and glory to Him that sits on the throne, and to the Lamb at His right hand. It is not possible ever to take away the ill desert of one who has sinned.

Most persons believe that our first parents were saved. Now when Adam disobeyed the command of God, and ate the forbidden fruit, perfectly aware at the time that he *was* disobeying God and was involving himself and his posterity in ruin, he had immediately a sense of his own ill desert, of his desert of punishment. But did he lose that sense of demerit when he became a penitent and when, by faith, he received the seed of the woman as his deliverer and Saviour? Not at all. Though peace came to his soul, yet he well knew and deeply *felt* that he richly merited death, spiritual and eternal. And now that he is as holy and happy as he was when first created in Eden, does he not feel, with overflowing gratitude to the Son of God his Saviour, that he enjoys what he by no means deserves to enjoy? Assuredly he does.

If when one becomes a convert his mind could be freed from confusion in regard to this matter, it might prevent him from receiving injury from erroneous teaching, and it might save him from having a morbid religious experience.

2. *We shall be of the greatest service to our young brethren in Christ if we can be the means of their obtaining, and also of their retaining clear views of that new relation (involved in their justification) which all true believers sustain to the law.*

One of the most difficult things which believers have to do, is to learn to exercise a steady unshaken confidence in the doctrine of gratuitous pardon, and yet the possession and exercise of this confidence is indispensable, in order that there may be real advancement in piety. It is the same thing as to clearly see the truth that the believer's relation to the law is changed — that he is justified freely by God's grace — that he is pardoned and accepted as righteous without being obliged to render a satisfaction to the law in his own person. To see and practically to believe the truth, moment by moment, that our relation to the law is changed; so changed that we have nothing to do in order to our pardon and acceptance—that we have only to receive pardon and acceptance gratefully, as a free gift, is, we say, difficult. And yet the new convert, who is so apt to make much of his frames, and so is in great danger of starting wrong, must learn the truth, and learn it so thoroughly that it shall shape his whole religious life. "To preach the doctrine of free grace fully," says an able writer, "without verging toward Antinomianism, is no easy task, and is, therefore, seldom done. But Christians cannot but be lean and feeble when deprived of their proper nutriment."

The apostle in teaching, in his epistle to the Romans, the doctrine of the believer's justification through Christ's righteousness, handles the subject of his freedom from the law separately, and illustrates it at the beginning of the seventh chapter.

Although no man can be a Christian who intelligently wishes to be subject to the law (as a rule of justification) in all its strictness, and who persists in striving to merit salvation by obedience to it, yet even the true Christian, and who consequently has no desire to be again under the law (*i. e.*, has no desire to be under obligation to obey the law as the condition of obtaining eternal life), has his times of conflict and anxiety, when he fears to venture wholly on Christ, and when he sinfully looks away from Him. At such times, forgetting that he has been made a partaker of the liberty wherewith Christ makes His people free, and goaded by his conscience, he endeavors to satisfy the law and gain the favor of God by meritorious acts, or by living a better life. This causes him to carry a heavy burden and hinders his progress in the divine life. Christians often show that they have not the consciousness which it is so necessary for them to have, of being free from the law as prescribing the condition on which eternal life is to be gained. They show this when they look upon their afflictions as a punishment. God never punishes His people, though in His faithfulness and love He often chastises them, and that severely. When believers think that God is punishing them—is sending evils upon them for no other purpose than to give them what they justly deserve—they make it manifest that they regard themselves not as free from the law but as subject to it. In the case of some Christians the only thing which prevents them from having an assurance of their own salvation is a vague thought which still lingers within them that their personal conformity to the law is the condition of their obtaining the favor of God and eternal life.

The attention of the young Christian should be directed to the fact that there is this tendency to legality in the heart, even in the believer's heart. "This is one of the phases of indwelling sin. Undoubtedly Christians are kept from a high degree of peace and joy in believing, because of their proneness to lose sight of Christ's vicarious righteousness, and to trust in personal righteousness. It should be noticed, however, that the true believer, in as far as he discovers this proneness and inclination, abhors it. He desires, above all things, to trust in Christ alone and perfectly, for justification. He is frequently, nay continually, foiled in regard not to a general and prevailing trust in

Him, but to a perfect and complete trust. He grieves over this fact, resists and fights with this inclination to self-righteousness and legality, and looks forward to an eternal rest in Christ, as his sacrifice for sin, and his righteousness before God. This lack of high and strong faith which characterizes us all, is owing to the remainders of corruption in us, and should be looked upon, and struggled with, just as indwelling sin generally should be." *

Converts cannot too soon be brought to understand the marvellous change which has taken place in their relation to that holy law of God which so lately condemned them. They cannot too soon be intelligently assured of the truth, that those sinners who believe in Jesus are free from the obligation to fulfil the law's demands in their own persons for the purpose of obtaining eternal life—that those sinners who believe in Jesus are now, " under a gracious dispensation according to which God dispenses pardon freely, and accepts the sinner as a sinner, for Christ's sake, without works or merits

---

* Dr. Shedd.

of his own." For until converts are brought to see and understand this doctrine, they must, of course, fail practically to feel it and act upon it, and then of what use can the blessed Saviour be to them? He cannot even be the author of their sanctification, for instead of remembering that growth in grace is secured by union to Christ, whereby we partake of his life, they will depend on their own strength to overcome sin. Moreover, as long as men are under a legal or slavish spirit, the principle of obedience in them is not love but fear. They cannot, therefore, have a filial spirit, and must be utter strangers to the Christian's happiness. "Their whole object is to propitiate God by means which they know to be inadequate. Their spirit is servile, their religion a bondage, their God a hard master. To men in such a state true love, true obedience, and real peace are alike impossible. There is no such thing as real acceptable obedience, until we are delivered from the bondage of the law as a rule of justification, and are reconciled to God by the death of His Son. Till then we are slaves and enemies and have the feelings of slaves. When we have accepted the terms of reconciliation we are the sons of God and have the feelings of sons."

It is necessary, then, that the convert should understand that all believers are entirely redeemed from the law; that they are, in perfect consistency with the holy character of God, justified in another way than by personally satisfying the law's demands; that God can be a just God and yet justify believers without exacting any righteousness which *they* have worked out; and that in the case of those who have already broken the law (and this is the case with believers), freedom from its demands, considered as prescribing the terms of acceptance, is necessary in order that their salvation may be a possible thing. He should be clearly taught that it is by the mystery of vicarious obedience and suffering, even by the satisfaction which the blessed Son of God rendered to law and justice as our substitute, and in our place, that we are delivered from the law's bondage. And, moreover, that this satisfaction rendered by the blessed Saviour, at the same time that it frees us from the obligation to obey and suffer in our own persons, constitutes the righteousness which is presented as the ground of our justification before God.

When a burdened and conscience-stricken member of the Romish Church is brought to see the utter falseness of the teaching of his Church concerning the way of salvation, and when he becomes enlightened as to the true way, how exceedingly, even beyond the power of words to express, does he prize this doctrine of the believer's freedom from the law! He had been taught that, although the removal from the soul of original sin is effected by baptism, and that, although grace is then infused, and guilt remitted, yet the sins which it is always committing after baptism cannot be perfectly forgiven until the process of sanctification within it is completed, that is, until the soul has at last reached thorough conformity to God's law, and is morally perfect. Then, and not before, can perfect forgiveness, and God's *entire* favor be enjoyed. But this sanctification (on the full completion of which God's entire favor depends) can only be carried on by being merited by the soul. Increase of grace must be deserved or merited by good works.

And, further, past sins must be atoned for by self-inflicted sufferings, in order that the grace lost through those past sins may be restored. Very few, however, attain to a state of Christian perfection in this life—most are still imperfect at death, while they have failed to make, by the pains of penance, sufficient satisfaction for their sins. These immediately after death go to purgatory, where they suffer by its fires more or less intensely for a longer or shorter period, until their sins are both atoned for and purged out. Thus perfection and the consequent favor of God can never be obtained, without being merited by ceaseless, slavish labor, and the endurance of dreadful suffering.

This way of being saved is the only one known to tens of thousands of sin-burdened souls. But now and then one who has long been in bondage to this cruel, legal system of Satan's devising, is delivered from his thraldom, is brought to see the light, and to know that he need not merit salvation, but that sinners who believe in Jesus are free from all the law's demands as the condition of enjoying God's favor, and are saved by grace, and entirely by grace. Is it easy to describe the joy of such a soul when it obtains its liberty, or to understand how precious the doctrine of the believer's freedom from the law must be to it!

As was said, the apostle, in treating the doctrine of the believer's justification in his epistle to the Romans, handles the subject of his freedom from the law separately, and, at the beginning of the seventh chapter illustrates it. He also, in the same epistle, strongly asserts the truth, as he does also in his epistle to the Galatians: "Ye are not under the law," he says, "but under grace." That is, your own personal obedience to the law is no longer the condition prescribed for your obtaining justification. You are under grace. Your justification is, as far as you are concerned, perfectly gratuitous.

Believers, then, from the very moment when by faith they are united to Christ, are free from the law. And further than this they are right before the law, viz., are forever justified, pronounced righteous, accepted on the ground of the Saviour's merits as fully entitled to the blessing of eternal life. Thus complete and wonderful is the change which has taken place in their relation to the law. But we should remember that the convert does not as yet fully realize the new and happy position which he occupies, and we should endeavor to instruct him concerning it. Unless he clearly understands it, he never can have a settled sense of forgiveness, nor the spirit of adoption, nor can he grow rapidly in grace.

3. *It should be made clear to the convert's mind that, although believers are free from the law in the sense that it is for them no longer the rule of justification, they sustain another relation to it which can never be terminated, but must always continue.*

There is no necessity that the convert should infer, if he is faithfully taught, that believers are in *every sense* free from the obligation to be conformed in their character and actions to the law. He can be taught that, in the sense of having liberty to sin, and to abstain from efforts to be holy, they never can be free. The apostle denies that any moral obligation is weakened by this deliverance of believers from the law. "What then?" he exclaims, "shall we sin, because we are not under the law, but under grace? God forbid. How shall we who died to sin, live any longer therein?"

While, then, sinners must be free from the law as a rule of justification if they are to be saved, no man can ever be free from it, as a rule of duty.

It should be made clear to the mind of the new believer that deliverance from the penalty is only a part of salvation, that Christ's death has become ours, not only as an expiation from sin, but even as a means of our sanctification. Indeed it is in order that we may be holy that we are pardoned, and the very reason why we are justified is that we may be sanctified. It is not mere pardon that is offered us in the gospel. "The very act by which we become interested in the redemption of Christ from the condemnation of the law makes us partakers of his Holy Spirit," who having renewed us in the whole man after the image of God, enables us more and more to die unto sin, and live unto righteousness.

There are those who have been, by an operation of the Holy Spirit, so changed as to their inward character, that it is now in some degree holy—in other words, is in some degree conformed to the requirements of God's holy law. Having been made holy, they love holiness. They fully recognize their obligation to be entirely free from sin, and they rejoice that this is required of them. They are well aware that they are only holy in part, but they are ever longing and striving to come up to the very standard of perfection. Nothing less can satisfy them. This is the only salvation they seek. "They feel that the charm and glory of redemption is deliverance from sin and conformity to God, that the whole design and purpose of the mission and sufferings of the Saviour would be frustrated if His people were not made partakers of His holiness. This is the crown of righteousness, the prize of the high calling of God, the exaltation and blessedness for which they long, and suffer, and pray."

Who are those who have experienced this blessed change in their nature, in their inward character, so that in character and life they are in some degree conformed to that law which is holy, just, and good, while they are constantly striving after more complete conformity to it? They are the very ones who in one sense are not under the law, who are so set free from it as a rule of justification that it no longer requires them to satisfy its demands as the condition of reaching heaven.

The convert who is brought to understand this, sees that two changes take place when one becomes a believer. His relation to the law is changed and there is also, by an operation of the Holy Spirit, such a change effected in his character that he is brought into a state of conformity (partial conformity) to the very law which no longer binds him as a rule of justification. At the same time he fully recognizes the fact that to be guilty of sin and to be wanting in perfect conformity to the Adamic law in all its extent and strictness, are precisely the same thing, and that therefore his obligation, to be completely conformed to it, must always remain. And while he recognizes this obligation, it gives him joy to think of it because he delights in the law of God after the inward man.

No true believer ever did, or ever will accept the dreadful Antinomian doctrine that holiness of life is not required of those to whom Christ's righteousness is imputed; that His people are delivered from all obligation to observe God's law, even as a rule of duty; that they are not bound to be personally conformed to it; that they are redeemed from it in *every* sense; that even should they continue in sin, they violate no law which they are bound to obey. We have already quoted the words of Paul in which he repudiates this horrible doctrine slanderously charged against him.

But while it is abhorrent to the mind of every true Christian to admit that God's law is abrogated, many whose piety we cannot doubt, maintain (at least in their creeds) that while a law does indeed exist, obedience to which is required, it is only the law which they call the evangelical law. No other law are believers required to obey. This, for Christ's sake, is substituted for the original law of absolute moral perfection, so that the latter is not now even our rule of action, to which it is our duty to be personally conformed. This milder law, Christ the mediator has introduced as being adopted to the fallen condition of man. It requires no more of men than that they should possess the conditions of faith and evangelical obedience, which condition all men are by grace made capable of fulfilling. These persons teach that God can consistently with His justice thus lower the demands upon us of the Adamic law, because Christ has fully satisfied its demands in our behalf. If obeying the evangelical law is the way to obtain justification, then the doctrine of perfection seems a necessary part of this scheme, and indeed its advocates hold that what they call gracious or Christian perfection is attainable, and is in fact actually attained by many before death. Although every true Christian whose creed contains even *this* system of belief, must reject the Antinomian doctrine, yet this system tends to Antinomianism, since by it the law of absolute perfection originally imposed on our race is set aside in order that the evangelical law may be substituted in its place.

Aspiration after complete conformity in character and life to God's perfect law, should possess the soul of every believer, and it would be well for converts if all their associations were always with Christians filled with this holy longing.

God's holy law is universal and immutable, and demands spotless holiness of every accountable being, and this because it is an expression of the absolute moral perfection of the divine nature. It should be impressed upon the mind of the convert that it can never be relaxed, and that not to come up to all its demands is to suffer infinite loss. He should be taught that the gospel even increases our obligations to be perfectly conformed to it. Never should he forget that although believers are, as has been shown, free from the law in the sense that it is for them no longer the rule of justification, they sustain another relation to it which must always continue.

4. *The convert needs instruction concerning the work of sanctification now begun in his soul.*

First, he needs to be taught that sanctification is as much due to the agency of the Holy Spirit as regeneration—that it is just as much a work of grace, and that it does not cease to be due to His agency because the soul exerts itself and co-operates in the process. Sanctification is not maintained solely by our own exertions, nor by the strength of the principle of grace communicated in regeneration; on the contrary, it is by the Spirit's agency all along, and from first to last, that any believer grows in holiness. Christians too often lose sight of this fact.

Second, that there could be no such thing as sanctification unless sin and holiness *both* existed in the soul. If regeneration removed *all* sin from the soul, then, after becoming in this way perfectly holy, it might continue to increase in holiness as the angels and the saints in heaven do; but *that* would not be sanctification. The very idea of sanctification supposes the existence of indwelling sin—a dying indeed unto it, but not a complete deliverance from it. In those who are the subjects of this work sin and holiness exist together.

Third. In the believer's sanctification sin becomes weaker and weaker, and its power is more and more destroyed, while holiness or spiritual life constantly grows and gradually triumphs over the principle of evil that still remains in the soul after its regeneration has taken place. And while in the main the good is victorious over the evil principle, the time approaches when it will be completely triumphant.

Fourth. The convert needs to be fully instructed in the truth that the blessed Saviour in whom the Holy Spirit dwells is the author of our sanctification *by communicating that same Holy Spirit to us.* Believers are united to Christ by faith, and, while one effect of this union is a participation in His merits, another effect is that we are made partakers of His Spirit—and are made partakers of His Holy Spirit expressly that this blessed Agent may carry forward the work of sanctification in our souls—expressly that He may dwell in us as a principle of life, to bring us more and more into conformity with the image of God.

Thus the convert may see *how* Christ is the author of our sanctification. The Holy Spirit, the third Person of the glorious Trinity, dwelling without measure in Christ, dwells also in us, so that we partake of Christ's life. Christ lives in us (Gal. ii. 20). We see in the Vine one of the illustrations presented to us in the Scriptures of the truth that believers participate in the life of Christ: "I am the vine, ye are the branches: he that abideth in me, and I in him, the same bringeth forth much fruit: for without me ye can do nothing." It must be deeply impressed on the mind of the convert that he can only be sanctified by Christ's living in him by His Holy Spirit—that in order to die unto sin and live unto righteousness, he must be strengthened with might by Christ's Holy Spirit in the inner man. Not that the divine Spirit accomplishes this work without employing the truth. He never acts independently of the Word, but always uses it as his instrument in producing holiness of heart and life. Its agency is asserted in such passages as these: "The engrafted word which is able to save your souls" (James i. 21). "The word of his grace which is able to build you up, and to give you an inheritance among all them that are sanctified" (Acts xx. 32). And the Saviour prays, "Sanctify them by thy truth, thy word is truth" (John xvii. 17). Still the truth could have no sanctifying, purifying effect did not the Holy Spirit attend it, work with it, and give it efficacy. During the believer's whole life His agency is necessary. Nor can sin be destroyed and spiritual life maintained and advanced in the soul in any way except by Christ living and abiding in it by His Spirit.

This is the scriptural explanation of the *manner* in which Christ is the Source of the believer's life; and it is a very different view from one which at the present day is having a wide acceptance. It is taught by some in these times that Christ wrought out and developed within Himself a holy frame and disposition which He had no need of for Himself any more than He had need of His merits which justify us, and that for our sanctification we must trust in Him for the impartation to us of this His inward holiness. According to this, we are sanctified by sharing His subjective righteousness by infusion through faith. And thus Christ is to do the whole work, and we have nothing more to do than passively believe that He will.

Fifth. Justification and sanctification are never separated in the believer's experience. Some maintain that the believer is by no means, as a matter of course, sanctified as soon as he is justified; that his sanctification does not begin when he first receives pardon. These persons teach that even after one has been regenerated and justified, years may pass before he enters upon the process of sanctification. When first converted, the soul accepts Christ for justification, then afterward, by a separate act, it accepts Him for sanctification. "In the ordinary and normal progress of the Christian life, after regeneration has taken place and after the soul has accepted Christ by faith as its Saviour from the condemnation and penalty of the law, there is a point at which it begins for the first time to believe in Christ for sanctification and becomes conscious of a transition into a new and higher state of life." Now, converts should be guarded against this error, and be taught that justification and sanctification, though they are to be distinguished, are never separated in experience —that true faith embraces Christ in all his offices as a complete Saviour from the guilt and power of sin. Forgiveness cannot be separated from purification. The blessed Jesus cannot be our Priest without being at the same time our Prophet and King; and the same act of faith which accepts Christ in one of his offices, accepts Him in all. The moment a man is justified by faith, that very moment the work of sanctification is begun in his soul.

Sixth. The absolute necessity, in order to its sanctification, of the vigorous co-operation of the soul itself with Him who works within it to will and to do. One would think that there is no necessity for dwelling on this. The humble, grateful convert, as we behold him, seems to know well that he himself must put forth effort. If he is truly a subject of God's grace he does not ask, Am I required to do anything? but *What* am I to do? He understands the teaching of the Scriptures as to the necessity of our working out our own salvation with fear and trembling, and he knows much about the means of grace which he is to use. Still he needs to be warned. So many have become slothful in spiritual things and relaxed their efforts, that we reasonably feel that each new convert is in danger of it. We co-operate with "God who worketh in us" when we feel the necessity of divine influence in order to our sanctification, and pray for it incessantly and with strong desires. Also when, in obedience to the command of Christ, we search the Scriptures and strive to obey their directions; when we faithfully use the public as well as the private means of grace, and we must not forget to add when we labor to do good to others.

5. If we seldom think of the Holy Spirit, and show no anxiety to become acquainted with what the Scriptures teach concerning Him, we are guilty of great sin, and need not expect to grow in grace. *The Spiritual good of the convert, therefore, requires that he be instructed concerning the doctrine of the Holy Spirit as it is revealed in the Bible.*

No true believer will deny the personality of the Holy Spirit. It is one thing, however, to admit His personality in words, and quite another to think of Him, feel toward Him, and pray to Him as a Person, who while He is the same in substance with the Father and the Son, is distinct from them. That He is in Himself a distinct, intelligent, and divine Person could not be more plainly taught in the Scriptures than it is.

Only a person can speak, and say I, and yet we are told (Acts xiii. 2) that "the Holy Ghost said, Separate *me* Barnabas and Saul for the work whereunto *I* have called them." In like manner the use of the pronoun He by our Saviour, when he speaks of the Holy Spirit, in the sixteenth chapter of John, as well as in other places, shows that the Holy Spirit is a person.

He sustains the relations to us, and performs the offices for us, of a teacher, comforter, and guide. Therefore, He is a Person.

He must be a person because the elements of personality, *i. e.*, intelligence, will, and individual subsistence, are expressly attributed to Him. They are attributed to Him in those passages in which He is said to search or know all things, even the deep things of God, and in which also He is said to will, and to act. I Cor. ii. 10, 12, and 1 Cor. xii. 11.

Since the Father and the Son are admitted to be distinct persons, the association of the Holy Spirit with them in our baptism shows that He also is a distinct person.

If the Holy Spirit is a divine Person, distinct from the Father and the Son, then to almost ignore Him as such, as some do who nevertheless profess to be His worshippers, is to be guilty of great sin. He demands of us recognition and honor.

The Holy Spirit is not the God-man. He did not subject Himself to the law which we broke, and become obedient unto death. He was not exalted to be the mediatorial King. It was the second person of the Godhead who was made of a woman, who was made under the law, who died for our sins, and who ascended to Heaven clothed in our nature, to sit at the right hand of God the Father. It is the son of man, while He is the Son of God, who, seated on His throne, nevertheless continues our great high Priest, and continually intercedes for us.

But while the blessed Spirit does not execute these offices for us, He has His own office work to perform in our redemption. All Christians are more or less familiar with the office of the Spirit in the work of redemption. They know that He created the body and soul of Christ, Matt. i. 18, 20. Luke i. 35, and that He replenished our Lord with all spiritual gifts, Isai. ii. 1, 2. They know that it is His office to reveal divine truth to men. All the Old Testament, and all the New Testament writers were the organs of the divine Spirit in the communication of God's will to a lost world. Not only did He reveal divine truth when He inspired holy men of old to write the Scriptures, but He is a revealer of the truth to the souls of men by giving them a sight, a perception of its glorious qualities. By rousing the moral nature of unrenewed men and giving activity to it He causes the truth of God's word which they read, or hear read, to have great power over them—power to restrain their wickedness within bounds, and to convict them of sin. All believers, also, know that it is the office of the Spirit to regenerate souls—to make converts, *i. e.*, to lead men to the exercise of faith and repentance, to take of the things of Christ and show them unto the soul, and to dwell in regenerated and believing men as a principle of a new divine and immortal life.

But, while it is probable that all true converts who live where Bibles abound, early obtain a knowledge of the office of the Holy Spirit in the work of redemption, there are still some things pertaining to His work, to His relation to us, and to our relation to Him, and also to our duties to Him, which are, perhaps, seldom taught them at an early stage of their Christian course.

I. They should be taught that the Holy Spirit is not only truly and strictly a Person equal in power and glory to the Father and the Son, but that He is a *free* Person, untrammelled by any laws which He has laid down to guide Himself by. Some seem to think that His influence is communicated according to fixed laws. The convert cannot too soon be taught the *voluntariness* of His agency. Then he will understand his dependence, and that of all men, on the blessed Spirit. Then he will not be likely to adopt erroneous views in regard to the way in which revivals are brought about. A respectable writer, speaking of revivals, foolishly says: "No one has yet succeeded in definitely stating *their law*, or bringing them under fixed conditions of time and circumstance." There is no law which controls the Holy Spirit, either in sending revivals, or in accompanying with power His truth, read or listened to *by the individual*. It is of the utmost importance that we should all feel our dependence on the good will of a *Person*. The influence of the Holy Spirit " is not the influence of a uniformly acting force co-operating with the truth; but that of a Person acting when and where He pleases; more at one time than at another, sometimes in one way, and sometimes in another."

2. We should all be deeply affected by the teachings of the Bible concerning those influences of the Spirit which (because He is kind to our world) He exerts on all unrenewed men. We should be grateful for those influences. This is a point to which the mind of the young believer should be directed, that he may early form the habit of recognizing the Spirit's *common* operations. There is not one out of the world of despair, who is not, in some degree, restrained by the Holy Spirit. We think men are bad, but what would they be if the Spirit of God should *entirely* withdraw from them as He does from the lost. "To the general influence of the Spirit we owe all the decorum, order, refinement, and virtue existing among men. Mere fear of future punishment, the natural sense of right, and the restraints of

human laws would prove feeble barriers to evil, were it not for the repressing power of the Spirit, which, like the pressure of the atmosphere, is universal and powerful, although unfelt." The reason why the Holy Spirit does not restrain men, and keep within bounds their corruptions *still more* than He does, is because believers do not continually pray that His *common* operations may be more powerful in our world.

3. The convert should be urged to bear in mind continually, that we live under the dispensation of the Spirit, and to endeavor to take in the full meaning of this truth. He is the one indispensable Agent in the whole work of the application of the redemption of Christ to lost men. Everything is subordinate to this chief gift of God, since Christ's ascension to the Father. " He is the Spirit of the Father, and He is the Spirit of the Son, and He is the Spirit of the believer, the one common Spirit of them all, by whom they are made one in that sublime and mystical fellowship set forth in the latter part of our Lord's intercessory prayer, John xvii. He is the life-giving Spirit

of souls dead in sin. He is the Spirit of conviction, of illumination, of sanctification, of consolation, of strength. He only reveals Christ in the soul, and transforms it into His image. On this sacred Person all men are absolutely dependent." It is the Spirit's work alone to conquer the world for Christ, by gathering souls into the Church. And, as the regenerating act is the act of the divine Spirit; so that instantaneous change in the soul by which it becomes *perfectly* holy in the article of death is effected by an act of the Holy Spirit alone.

4. In addition to what has been said, there is a certain caution and a certain entreaty which should, with great earnestness, be addressed to converts. They should be *cautioned* to avoid everything which would grieve the blessed Spirit, since we cannot grieve Him without being in imminent danger of losing His influences. It is easy to learn what *does* grieve Him. Only let the soul be constantly afraid of wounding and offending this infinitely condescending, gracious, and powerful Friend, and the danger of committing this sin will be greatly lessened. The *entreaty* is, that they

not only pray for the Holy Spirit, but that they ask that they may be *filled* with Him. Some saints receive this gift in larger measure than others, because they pray more for it. We should never be satisfied with what we now possess of the Spirit's presence and influences. Our Heavenly Father does not wish us to be- Our desires for this priceless blessing should be absolutely insatiable.

6. It should be deeply impressed upon the mind of the young disciple, *that the gospel is represented in the Scriptures under the form of a covenant*, and that it is so called by Christ Himself (Mat. xxvi. 28). The Saviour promises us the salvation of our souls, and we promise the blessed Saviour, in His strength, faith and obedience. Here is a covenant between Christ and the believer. At first we embrace this covenant in the secrecy of our souls, namely, by exercising faith, which is an inward act. Then, when we are baptized, we embrace it outwardly and visibly.

All Christians know that the Scriptures use the word covenant, in setting forth the way of salvation, but few seem to be aware of the frequency with which they employ it. The word should be dear to us, not only because it is in the Bible, but because the Holy Spirit, who is the author of the Scriptures, uses it so often. Christians should be just as familiar with the word covenant, as they are with the words "grace," "throne of grace," "heirs of the promise," "kingdom of God," "redemption," "precious faith," etc.

Why do the Scriptures so prominently represent the gospel under this form? One reason undoubtedly is, to lead us constantly to bear in mind the fact that we must co-operate with God (in ways already pointed out) in the work of our salvation. When two persons enter into a covenant, each has conditions to perform. And so if Christ and the believer have covenanted with each other, not only has the condescending Saviour conditions to fulfil, but so has the believer. The Saviour will be faithful to His covenant-promise, which is to save us on condition that He continues to find in us faith and obedience to the very end. We must see to it that we, also, are faithful to our engagements. Otherwise we are covenant-breakers, and by the very terms of the covenant (which require co-operation on our part) salvation must be withheld from us.

This covenant between Christ and His people is not made once for all. It is constantly renewed. It is secretly renewed in every act of faith, and it is renewed publicly whenever we partake of the Lord's Supper. Let the convert be well instructed as to the existence and the nature of this covenant, and let him daily remember what the Bible teaches concerning it, and he may expect to be, all his life, a better Christian in consequence. If he is a parent let him remember, with gratitude, that it includes his children, so that its precious promises are meant also for them.

We have now presented some of the truths which the inspired writers of the Scriptures clearly and powerfully set forth, and seek to impress upon all classes of believers. If we are the means, by our instructions and example, of bringing converts to know and act upon these truths, we cannot but greatly benefit them. They may be expected to have a healthy religious experience, to grow in grace, and to be useful members of the Church of Christ.

CHAPTER IV.

SOME OF THE CHRISTIAN'S DUTIES, DIFFICULTIES, PRIVILEGES AND ACTIVITIES, IN REGARD TO WHICH THE CONVERT NEEDS TO BE INSTRUCTED.

DUTIES.

DUTIES which are also graces of the Spirit.—As in exercising the Christian graces we co-operate with the Holy Spirit; as they are capable of being cultivated, and as they are only different ways in which our souls act in obeying God and serving men, they are duties as well as Christian graces. Now the convert needs to be instructed in regard to these duties. He should know what the Bible says about them. It speaks of them all, and some of them it dwells upon fully. Even the most careless reader of the Scriptures knows how much they dwell upon the grace of faith, and how incessantly they demand it of us as a duty.

They insist likewise on the duty of exercising love. They speak of the love which is due to Christ, and command us to love the saints, strangers, enemies, and all men. They tell us that we ought to manifest this love by clothing the naked, visiting the sick, sympathizing with the afflicted, covering the faults of others, and forgiving injuries. They command us to practise the duty and grace of self-denial whenever our desires are evil in their nature, or when, though they may be innocent in themselves, they become sinful by being immoderate. They also teach us to practise the duty of self-denial whenever the gratification of our own wishes is inconsistent with the good of others. As for the duty and grace of liberality we find exhortations to it in Luke iii. 11, xi. 41 ; Acts xx. 35 ; 1 Cor. xvi. 1 ; 1 Tim. vi. 17, 18. Precious promises are made to liberality, and blessings are connected with it in Psalm cxii. 9; Prov. xi. 25, xxviii. 27 ; Eccle. xi. 1, 2 ; Isa. lviii. 10 ; Psalm xli. 1 ; Prov. xxii. 9. We are to exercise liberality toward saints, the poor, strangers, all men, even enemies, in lending to those in want, and by forwarding missions.

We are to give without ostentation, with simplicity, according to ability, and willingly. We are assured that if we give cheerfully, God will love us, 2 Cor. ix. 6, 7. In order to stimulate us to liberality, the Scriptures present to us many exemplifications of it. See especially 2 Cor. viii. 1-5.

We should remember that all that we call our own, really belongs to the Lord Jesus, and that not only because He is God and the Creator and proprietor of all things, but because He is Mediatorial King. All things have been given by the Father to His Son Jesus, the God-man, that Jesus may make all tributary to the advancement of His kingdom. But He could not cause all things that exist to concur in the execution of this glorious design unless they were given to him in such a sense as to belong to him, in such a sense as to be his own. What we call our own, then, is only *apparently* ours—really it belongs to our Lord Jesus, that He may use it to further the interests of His kingdom. By His Father's gift He is the possessor of the universe, with the creatures that live in it—rational and irrational, and with whatever they fondly look upon as their own. The blessed Jesus then possesses our money, our dwellings, our farms, our merchandise, our books, and our ornaments, and even our food and clothing are His. What, then, is there so very commendable in giving, or rather *returning* to Him the money which is already His, that it may be employed to build up His glorious kingdom? It is His loving kindness to us which causes Him to look upon our contributions in the light of gifts, and to reward us for making our contributions to His cause. The convert should be taught to view the matter thus, and to form the habit of doing so.

Among the characteristics of the Christian which are both duties and graces, the Bible mentions "bowels of mercies, kindness, humbleness of mind, meekness, long-suffering; forbearing one another, and forgiving one another, as Christ forgave us, together with charity, which is the bond of perfectness," Col. iii. 12–14. The convert should be taught that he is to co-operate with the Holy Spirit in exercising these.

Secret duties.—The devotional reading of the

Scriptures and closet prayer are the principal duties to be performed in secret. Both should be faithfully attended to. Both are means of grace. If they are but little prized and carelessly attended to by the believer at the commencement of his course they are likely to be neglected ever afterward.

There is much about prayer which the convert and the advanced believer know in common. Both know that while God commands us to pray, it is infinite condescension in Him to permit us to have communion with Him. Both know that no one can be a Christian who never prays—that prayer is as essential to the spiritual life as the heart's pulsations are essential to the natural life. Both know that prayer is speaking to God, and that in it we confess sin, offer supplications, and express the feelings of love, adoration, and gratitude. Both know that one needs not be perfect before he can pray, but that prayer is an act of a sinner; that the precise thing asked for is not always granted even when the prayer is acceptable to God and brings a blessing; and that he who regards iniquity in his heart will not be heard.

But, while the advanced Christian and the convert alike understand these things, the older Christian knows better than the new convert does that prayer helps the soul onward in the Christian life; that if, in times of temptation to despondency or sin, it prays fervently, it is "conscious of a strength to resist or to endure, which no effort of will, and no influence of motives, ever could impart;" that prayer is powerful to comfort, calm, lighten, and strengthen the distressed soul; that, if one is conscious of a reluctance to engage in the act, he must not wait until a spirit of prayer comes over him, but must ask, and seek, and knock, and expect a blessing from God in the use of His appointed means; that it is possible for the habit of prayer to be so strengthened that the act cannot be omitted without pain; and that the Holy Spirit assists those who are faithful in attending to the duty. Now, whatever the more experienced believer has learned concerning prayer, he should be anxious to teach his younger brother.

It would be an unspeakable benefit to the new convert could he be brought to feel the importance of having fixed regular times set apart for the purpose of praying in his closet. There is reason to believe that habits of systematic prayer are seldom persevered in, unless they are begun when one is first converted. Nor should these prayers of stated seasons and of the closet be very brief. When we withdraw from the world and set ourselves in the presence of God, we cannot always be warmed and revived in a moment. During the first few moments the thoughts are apt to wander, so that if we rise from our knees shortly after commencing our devotions we fail to reap the benefit of them. Let secret prayer be prolonged, and then penitence, and love, and all holy affections will at last manifest their existence. "No external activity, though pushed to the utmost, can make up for the want of closet devotion. If we would learn how Elijah, Daniel, Paul, Augustine, Luther, Whitefield, Martyr, Payson, and Judson came to quit themselves like men, we must accompany them to their wrestling prayers. The world has half destroyed us when we are too busy to pray. In closet devotion, unless it be formal, scanty, or hurried, the young Christian comes to the feet of the Lord, touches the hem of His garment, has communion with Him in regard to all his offices and divine graces. Such converse with God, especially over the inspired volume, secures against defection and error, procures pardons, sprinkling of the expiatory blood, and the Spirit of adoption; mortifies secret lurking, insidious sins; quickens the pulse of zeal and the pace of service; arms for battle, lifts the courage, and sweetens the cross."

When we read the Scriptures we find that the Christian soldier is expected not merely to use oral prayer in his closet, but to be very frequently employed in offering up mental and ejaculatory prayers. Thus the apostle says, in the 2d chapter of his Epistle to the Ephesians: "Stand, therefore, ... and take the sword of the Spirit, which is the word of God, praying always with all prayer and supplication." God's people may and should commune with Him in their hearts during the busy hours of the day. When surrounded, moreover, by the social circle, when seeking recreation, when walking the streets, when pursuing their journeys, when reading and studying, and when at their meals, their hearts should often go out after God, and they should inwardly beg His blessing, His help, His protection and guidance, and His Holy Spirit. Our blessed Redeemer tells us that men ought always to pray ; and, if we had a constant sense of God's nearness to us, and of our great necessities, we would thus pray.

Another direction in regard to the duty of prayer, which should be given to converts, is, that they make supplication to God not with reference to great and important matters only, but with reference to matters which we are apt to look upon as of trifling import. This would only be obeying the injunction of the apostle, "Be careful for nothing ; but in everything by prayer and supplication, with thanksgiving, let your requests be made known unto God." How often is it the case that, simply because the source of our anxiety seems of small moment, we are averse to asking for help and deliverance ; whereas, the apostle says, "in everything." Then, again, we are apt to decide, to plan, and to act, with reference to our family and business affairs, and even with reference to matters pertaining to Christ's kingdom, without seeking guidance and wisdom from above ;

whereas, God's Word says, "Lean not to thine own understanding, in all thy ways acknowledge Him, and He will direct thy steps." "If I have any affair," says Cecil, "to transact with another, I must pray that God would be with us in that affair, lest we should blunder, and injure, and ruin each other." We should also pray daily for common mercies, which come regularly from the hand of God. Though we always expect to receive our daily bread, yet we should ever pray for it. When we forget our dependence on our Heavenly Father for these mercies, they are often withheld from us.

Social duties.—The social duties which are of a devotional nature are those of attending the prayer-meeting, and of worshipping God in the Sanctuary. The convert cannot be too earnestly warned that, as regards neglecting these duties, the very beginnings of neglect are full of danger. "He should be taught to magnify preaching and prayer-meetings, and positively to abhor the excuses made by so many for neglect and absence."

There are social duties besides those of a *devotional* nature, concerning which the Scriptures give much instruction, but on these we have not space to dwell.

Other duties deserving of mention will be considered when we come to speak of Christian activities.

DIFFICULTIES.

We have mentioned some of the duties required of Christ's disciples. In speaking now of the difficulties of living the Christian life, it would be proper to class among them the daily practice of these duties. In practising them there is indeed great reward, and yet it is no easy thing to do. The tendency to indolence must be resisted. The soul must constantly rouse itself to action. It must be energetic. It must put forth as great effort, as if everything depended upon its own exertions, and yet it must rely as fully and earnestly on God's help, as if no co-operation on its own part was required. Well does the Christian know that he will fail to perform his duties, unless he exerts himself vigorously, while at the same time he relies continually on God to work within him, and he will earnestly desire that in regard to so important a truth, his young brethren should reap the benefit of his own experience.

Conflicts with spiritual enemies may also be classed among the Christian's trials and difficulties. As to the opposition he experiences from his spiritual enemies the convert is in a new world. It is true that Satan and the world have never in any time past been his real friends; they have always been enemies to his salvation. They have, however, hitherto permitted him to live in peace. But now that he has left their service and enlisted in the service of the Saviour, their deadly hatred and opposition to him and his course are fully aroused. And it is only by going back to the world and by yielding to Satan's yoke again, that he can cease to be tormented by their opposition. He has then begun a life of conflict which is attended with all the more danger to himself because it is new to him. For his warfare having but recently begun he is inexperienced in it. He has not the strength and the wisdom which are so important to enable him to resist his enemies perseveringly and successfully, and to enable him also to understand and escape their wiles. His situation, therefore, should awaken our deepest interest in him, and we should be fully alive to the fact that he needs all the help we can give him.

The only way in which our spiritual enemies can succeed in injuring us is by tempting us. Depravity is not entirely destroyed when the soul is regenerated. The principle of evil still exists within the soul, and it has great power. Our sinful thoughts and feelings are only the actings of this principle of evil—this depraved nature. Thus we are continually sinning without any temptations to sin. But we would not commit as many sins as we do, if we were never tempted. There is no compulsion. Temptations have no compelling power. They do not force us to sin. When they prevail, therefore, we are not innocent and excusable. Still we are constantly sinning under their influence. Now the new convert needs to be instructed in regard to those temptations or solicitations to evil which every advanced Christian is so familiar with.

Our affections and desires must have some objects to terminate on, and the world tempts us by presenting objects to excite our inordinate or unholy affections and desires, as its honors and pleasures. Large numbers yield to these allurements of the world, pursue the world's riches and honors, and are lost. The world also tempts the timid by its threats. These threatenings of the world's contempt and hatred are often more dreaded than death. Of course the world would have but little power to tempt were there no sin within us— were there no pride, envy, self-seeking, covetousness, ambition, sensuality, malice, etc., to act upon. Satan and the world depend for their success on the depravity within us. For Satan is our great tempter. He does not act alone. All fallen spirits are his subordinates, and he employs them all. Satan's power, and that of the evil spirits under him, to tempt, is dreadful. Repeatedly do the Scriptures caution the people of Christ against Satan's devices. They teach us that Satan never sleeps, that he takes us when we are off our guard, and that his temptations are subtle and hard to be detected. It is fearful to think that no Christian ever passes a long time without being tempted by Satan, but it is comforting to know that our Saviour is infinitely more powerful than he is, and that He is willing to protect us from being tempted and to deliver us when temptation comes. But besides appealing to Christ as our Saviour, our King, to protect us, we are to use those means of resistance —those weapons described in Eph. vi. 11-18.

The afflictions which are peculiar to the Christian make it difficult for the believer to live in such a way as to glorify the Saviour and make His religion lovely in the eyes of the world. Therefore, the Christian's *afflictions* should be mentioned in any enumeration which may be made of the believer's difficulties, since there is great danger that while pressed down by them, he will manifest an unsubmissive and unbelieving spirit. That it is necessary that Christ's people should suffer is plainly taught us. "If so be that we suffer with Him," says the apostle, writing to the Roman Christians. "Beloved," says the Apostle Peter, "think it not strange concerning the fiery trial which is to try you: as though some strange thing happened unto you, but rejoice, inasmuch as ye are partakers of Christ's sufferings ; that, when His glory shall be revealed, ye may be glad also with exceeding joy." Thus it appears that we shall not share with Christ in His exaltation and glory, unless we are partakers of His sufferings. But the new convert, if left to himself, will not speedily learn how to interpret afflictions, nor how to behave under them, nor how to use them. If you yourself have been measurably faithful in following Christ you understand more about the peculiar trials of God's people than young believers do, and are in some degree competent to be of service to them.

Ministers of the gospel too often pursue a different course in their efforts to aid converts from that which our Saviour and the apostles took. They give little warning of the trials through which God calls all His people to pass. "If any man," says our Lord, "will be my disciple, let him deny himself, and take up his cross, and follow me." And the apostle warned his converts that they must "through much tribulation enter into the kingdom of God." But it may be asked, why should we, in the commencement of the Christian life, be told of coming trials which may discourage us. The answer to this is, that in the matter of being Christ's disciples it is better to count the cost in the very outset. When we know beforehand what we must encounter, we shall be better prepared for the difficulties which lie in the way, than if we start with false expectations. Besides, the service of Christ is a willing service, and this requires that the true state of the case should be fairly presented. It would, indeed, be contrary to the teachings of the Bible and also to the experience of God's people to affirm that a holy life is an unhappy one. None know what true happiness is except Christians. But to endure the afflictions which are the peculiar experience of God's children is perfectly compatible with the possession of that peace which the world knows not of.

While the convert is plainly warned by the Saviour and His inspired servants of the difficulties and dangers which will beset his path, he is also encouraged by many promises. He is assured that the diligent use of the means of grace shall certainly be rewarded with success, and that the faithful servant of Jesus shall continually have the sympathy, approval, and presence of the Master, and the powerful aids of the Holy Spirit.

PRIVILEGES AND SPIRITUAL GIFTS.

Love, faith, self-knowledge, a heart to forgive enemies, a spirit of prayer, of liberality, and of self-denial are, as has been already said, Christian duties. But they are also gifts. A knowledge of self must not be considered an exception. It *also* is a gift. It is as much a gift of the Holy Spirit as faith or love. It consists mainly in a sense of indwelling sin. The true believer does not dread to possess this knowledge or consciousness of his inward pollution and sinful weakness. On the contrary he is grateful to the Holy Spirit for enabling him to see his own vileness. He mourns to think of the deceitfulness of his heart which so long prevented him from perceiving the depth of the iniquity lodged within him. He desires to be less deceived than he even *still* is—in other words to have his sense of his sinfulness deepened, because he loves all truth even the real truth about himself. Another reason why he desires to grow in the knowledge of his vileness and ill desert is because such growth (as he has learned by experience) is accompanied with increasing love to Jesus. It is accompanied with steadily increasing love and gratitude to Jesus, while it is not attended with the least fear of suffering the punishment deserved.

The indwelling sin of which the believer is conscious, occupies—if he is a spiritually minded Christian—much of his attention, and he is constantly confessing it to God. But the love to God, and trust in Jesus which he is also conscious that he possesses, occupy but little of his attention. He feels no inclination to contemplate them, much less to admire them. Still, it is a great blessing to have a vivid consciousness of their existence, because this is one of the ways by which the Christian obtains an assurance of his own salvation, though it is true that he mainly rests his assurance on what is out of himself and not on what he finds within himself.

In regard to this gift or privilege, which all

converts should desire to possess—the privilege sometimes called the full assurance of hope—we have several things to say. (1.) It is enjoyed by some from the very beginning of their Christian course. In the case of some the Holy Spirit bears witness with their spirits that they are children of God, even when they are first regenerated. There is no certainty, however, that they will not lose their assurance unless they continue to use the means of grace with energy—to be very prayerful, watchful, and diligent in practising universal holiness. The Protestant Reformers never seem to have lost that assurance of their own salvation, which was given them at the time of their conversion. (2.) One may be a true believer without possessing this gift; *i.e.*, full assurance is not of the essence of faith. Let it be understood what we mean to deny, and what we intend to affirm by this proposition. I deny that if I trust in Jesus to save me an *assurance* that He loves me is essential to this trust. But I do not deny, but affirm, that *some degree of belief* that He loves me *is* essential to the existence of this trust. And my feeble belief that I am the object of His love will rise to an assurance of it when my trust in Him as my Saviour becomes very vigorous. Our Catechism defines faith in Jesus Christ to be a saving grace, whereby we rest upon Christ for salvation. Now how can I truly rest upon Christ for my salvation without having a *particle* of belief that I am an object of His love. To be *totally* destitute of belief in His love for me, and yet to rest even feebly upon Him to save me is an impossibility. But, as was said, a *full assurance* that He loves us does not *necessarily* enter into our faith—in other words, is not essential to the existence of faith, as is proved by the experience of very many of God's people. (3.) Some are quite confident that they are in the favor of God and estate of salvation, who are mistaken notwithstanding. "That unregenerate men, beguiled by the natural desire for happiness, flattered by self-love, and betrayed by a spirit of self-righteousness, and self-confidence, should sometimes indulge an unfounded assurance of their own gracious condition, is rendered antecedently probable from what we know of human nature, and rendered certain as a fact from common observation, and from the declarations of Scripture." (4.) The attainment of this assurance is a Christian duty. It is made a duty in Scripture. In Heb. vi. 11, we are exhorted "to show the same diligence to the full assurance of hope unto the end." We are convinced that its attainment is a duty, when we consider also what naturally and inevitably accompanies it—desires for still more intimate fellowship with God, increased diligence in efforts to obey and glorify the Saviour, humility, gratitude, and liberation from that anxiety about our *own* spiritual state which stands in the way of our helping others. (5.) The directions which we would give to converts as to the way of arriving at a full assurance of their own salvation are these :

First. Obtain clear views of the way of salvation, especially of the truth that believers in Christ are free from the law as prescribing the terms of acceptance with God, while the Saviour's righteousness avails to justify them ; they being bound now and forever to obey the perfect law as a rule of duty. Contemplate these truths long and often, with prayer, that they may command your full and joyful acquiescence, and may never be lost sight of.

Second. Remember that what authorizes us to come to Christ is not any peculiar experience which we may have in our souls, but God's free, perfectly generous, unconditional promise to accept all coming sinners—that when we wait until we find in ourselves some peculiar experience as our warrant for coming, we just hinder ourselves from being saved. And, remembering this, come (the coming is to be constantly repeated), RELYING on this promise as thus perfectly free and unconditional.

Third. Since your *trust in Christ* is capable of being greatly strengthened, use every means to strengthen it pointed out by the inspired writers, especially prayer. For, as soon as your grasp of Christ is a powerful grasp, you will have not a faint belief, but a full assurance that he loves you.

Fourth. Make much of the verse, Rom v. 5, where we are told that the Holy Spirit produces in the believer an immediate consciousness that he is the object of God's love. The words in that verse are, " And hope maketh not ashamed, because the love of God [God's love to us] is shed abroad in our hearts by the Holy Ghost which is given unto us." Pray very importunately that the Holy Spirit would give you this inward persuasion that God loves you. Ask until you receive.

Fifth. Grow in grace, in order to which be exceedingly diligent in using the means of grace.

It was said that when faith, the faith which has Christ for its object, the faith which truly lays hold upon Him, is exceedingly strong and active, there will be a full assurance of His love. How precious then is this faith! What can we more earnestly desire than that it should not only be preserved, but daily increase in power. It is, however, the special work of the Holy Spirit to watch over this life-giving faith in Jesus, to nourish it, and make it more and more vigorous. Let every convert, then, unweariedly and importunately entreat his Heavenly Father to give His Holy Spirit, pleading His own promise to give this blessing to those who ask Him. We have already said that the witnessing of the Spirit, the shedding abroad by the Spirit of God's love in the heart, must be sought by prayer. In no other way can the witnessing of the divine Comforter be obtained.

In regard to a full assurance of salvation, we think some sad mistakes are made by many.

1. It is a mistake to suppose that the piety of those who enjoy a full assurance is different in its nature from the piety of those who have not attained to an assurance. It is claimed by a certain class of Christians that their religious experience has undergone such a change that they now have no occasion to cry "Who shall deliver me from the body of this death!" They have passed out of the bondage of the seventh chapter of the epistle to the Romans into the sweet liberty of the eighth. They are inwardly conscious that they exercise a *new* faith which receives Christ for everything. Only to those who possess this new faith—who have thus entered "by the right principle upon the process of sanctification," can the full assurance of their own salvation belong. Thus, the spiritual life of those who have this inward certainty differs in kind from that of those who have it not.

The very statement of this error is its own refutation. We all feel that the life of God in the soul of one believer is necessarily the same that it is in the souls of all other believers. All who are united to Christ by the indwelling of the Holy Spirit possess the same life which abides in Him. But all believers are united to Christ by the indwelling of the Holy Spirit; and therefore all believers, those assured of their own salvation and those without this assurance, have precisely the same life.

2. It is a mistake to feel certain that only a few believers possess assurance.

Did we know that a very great degree of piety is essential to its possession, there might be some reason for our having this certainty. But the Holy Spirit can give assurance to one in whom spiritual life is not remarkably vigorous, and this assurance thus bestowed may lead to greater attainments in holiness. Doubtless many Christians of great experience and deep piety often have anxiety and fears which many who are less holy are free from. At any rate, there are thousands of truly contrite souls, and to whom the Saviour will say in that day, "Come, ye blessed of my Father," whose future prospects are obscured because of their doubts respecting their own spiritual condition; while there may be many inferior to these in experience and depth of piety, but who have the simple, implicit faith of little children, accompanied with assurance of hope.

3. It is a mistake to suppose that it is unsafe and even dangerous for Christians to be assured of their own salvation.

The enjoyment of assurance would, indeed, be unsafe and injurious, did it have a tendency, as some suppose it has, to lead to carelessness, inattention to the duties of religion, pride, or presumption. But it has no such tendency. In the case of true Christians, genuine assurance leads to unfeigned humility, increased diligence in the practice of holiness, and constant longings after more intimate fellowship with God. It is only when assurance is spurious that its effects are self-righteousness, neglect of duty, indulgence in sin, hardness of heart, and selfishness. Let no one suppose that either ardent love for Jesus, lively gratitude for salvation, tender pity for the perishing, or any other fruit of holiness, will be wanting in one who is fully assured of God's love for him, provided his assurance is produced by the Holy Spirit.

It would, also, be attended with loss to its possessor, did it cause him to be in a great measure exempt from affliction. There are graces which could never be exercised, except under affliction. God sends trials upon all His people, because it is necessary that they should experience them. Assurance has no tendency to dull, natural sensibility.

Nor could any one, without injury to himself, be in possession of this gift or privilege, did it have the effect of turning away his attention from the sin which dwells within him. Some appear to think that assurance has this effect, and, indeed, it would seem as if the very reason why they value it so highly, is the fact that it introduces its possessor, as they suppose, into a state in which, if there *is* any sin remaining within him, it no longer afflicts him. But one feeling his own exceeding sinfulness may be burdened, grieved, afflicted without having any alarm or painful fears of suffering the penalty due to sin. If I am assured that Jesus loves me, and will never cease to love me—that even while I am here in the body, my perfect salvation has had its beginning, and, that now I am forever safe, it is impossible for me to be distressed by fears that sin will ever triumph over me. I know it never will. I even know that the time is near when I shall be made perfect in holiness. But I may still—indeed, I *must* still—be burdened and afflicted by the consciousness of indwelling corruption. If I am deeply in love with holiness, and truly hate sin, how can my assurance of my own salvation make me cease to grieve that that which I hate is ever present with me, is ever within me. I must be afflicted, and there will be times when I shall be *full* of sorrow. " Although the regenerate believer is not in the total and hopeless slavery of the unregenerate man, he is yet under so much of a bondage as to prevent perfect obedience ; to make him poor in spirit, ' weary and heavy laden,' and to force from him the cry: ' O, wretched man, who shall deliver me ?'"* If the principle of holiness, and the principle of sin exist together in the

---

* Dr. Shedd's "Com. on Romans."

soul, they must oppose each other; there must be a "warring," Rom. vii. 23; the believer's whole life must be a conflict. But even while he struggles against sin he can exclaim: " I thank God through Jesus Christ, our Lord," because he knows that this conflict is not to result in the victory of sin, but in the triumph of grace. Some seem to think that to be conscious of indwelling sin, and to feel, with much grief, its great power, *is the same* as to be under condemnation," whereas one of the strongest proofs that a man is *free* from condemnation, is that he not only admits in words, that sin dwells within him, but is deeply conscious of it, is burdened by it, and perseveringly struggles against it.

It is not, then, attended with danger or any evil whatever for a true believer to have an assurance of his own salvation.

4. It is a mistake to suppose that, where one has spiritual life abiding within him, the best way for him to arrive at an assurance of it is to look *within* for the purpose of examining his own heart. At the very time when he is looking *away* from himself to Christ, and is dwell-

ing long and constantly on the sweetness, glory, and loveliness of Jesus, and on His infinite kindness and grace, he may have in his soul a consciousness that he loves Christ, and an assurance that Christ loves him. You are, indeed, commanded to examine yourself, and you must obey the command. But where did you ever learn, that when the apostle, or rather the Holy Spirit sets this duty before us, he meant that it is to be performed by looking within, by acts of introspection. There are much better ways of examining ourselves than that. If our object in examining ourselves is to see whether we are Christians or not, we should, instead of analyzing our *experiences*, inquire whether we love and worship Jesus as God, receive His doctrines, trust in His sacrifice and intercession, obey, trust in, and serve Him as our King. We shall be assisted to answer these questions, if we place the divine object of the Christian's faith and love before our minds, and contemplate His Person, His perfections, His wonderful, sweet condescension and love. As for examining ourselves to see whether our conduct be consistent, and our motives pure, and whether our progress in the divine life is what it ought to be, *that* should be a daily exercise. We should call ourselves to account every day, to see where we have failed.*

5. It is a mistake to suppose that, unless one has a settled assurance, he never can have moments of gladness and peace.

Even believers who are not fully assured of their salvation have received a new nature, have been justified, and made the children of God, and joint heirs with Christ of eternal glory. They, therefore, cannot be destitute of comfort. They have more or less of the spirit of adoption. They often enjoy prayer. There are times when their graces are in lively exercise. They are happy in doing good, and they enjoy the society of their fellow Christians.

It seems unnecessary to spend any time in pointing out the advantages which those believers who enjoy this assurance have over those who are destitute of it. No man or angel ever did or ever will enjoy a greater good than to

---

* Dr. Hodge's "Conference Papers."

be loved by Christ. How delightful and animating, then, to have a perfect assurance in my soul that He loves me, provided this assurance is not spurious, but is produced by the Holy Spirit. Besides, is it not natural to suppose that the Christian who possesses this assurance will oftener than others have spiritual peace and joy, great love and thankfulness to God, and buoyancy, strength, and cheerfulness in the practice of obedience in every department of duty? No wonder the Bible commands all to strive to possess this gift. Let no convert put off using the means to secure it. Nothing is gained by delay. No one has a right to tell you that you must wait long before the blessing can be yours.

That Bunyan believed in the possibility of even new converts possessing a full assurance of their acceptance, is evident from what he says of Christian's roll, given him by one of the shining ones soon after he began his pilgrimage. It will be remembered that when Christian came up to the cross his burden loosed from off his shoulders and fell from him. Then he stood awhile to look and wonder. "Now," says Bunyan, "as he stood looking and weeping, behold three shining ones came to him and saluted him with 'Peace be to thee.' So the first said to him: 'Thy sins be forgiven thee;' the second stripped him of his rags and clothed him with a change of raiment; the third also set a mark on his forehead, and gave him a roll with a seal upon it, which he bid him look on as he ran, and that he should give it in at the Celestial Gate." It was because this roll was the assurance of his life and acceptance, that he so greatly bewailed its loss through his sinful sleep at the pleasant arbor.

We are on the subject of the Christian's privileges, which all converts should desire to possess, and the one on which we have chiefly dwelt is that of an assurance of salvation. In addition to this there are privileges which many—both those who have received, and those who have not received an assurance of their own salvation—enjoy, as, great liberty in prayer; clear, spiritual discernment; frequent gracious promptings, and movements of the indwelling Spirit; strength to yield to those promptings and thus to avoid grieving the Spirit; great ease and readiness in interceding for others; the power of turning the thought Godward and heavenward; deliverance from fear of death; wisdom in counselling and comforting others in their spiritual difficulties; the happiness of being the objects of the love of the most spiritually minded, etc. When we have power given us to see things of a temporal nature in their true light, in the light of the Bible, in the light of eternity, in the light in which God and angels look upon them, we are highly favored and enjoy a great privilege. We are highly privileged when the Holy Spirit enables us to glory in infirmities— to see that our afflictions which weigh us down, are working out for us a far more exceeding and eternal weight of glory.

The more closely we walk with God the greater are our privileges.

The high privileges of the believer are within the reach of all God's people, and the attention of converts should be called to them, and they should endeavor to attain them and should be encouraged to do so.

ACTIVITIES.

The convert is not sufficiently aware of the importance of beginning to exert himself at once for the good of others. His life flows in one current. He is apt to be engrossed in one thing. It is characteristic of converts to be much absorbed in their own happiness and blessedness. They forget that in a good sense they are now to be proselyters. This truth was understood by the first converts. So active in efforts to save their fellow men were the hundred and twenty disciples in Jerusalem (Acts i. 15) that before the lapse of many years, Christ's disciples were numerous in all parts of the Roman Empire. Many suppose that Christ's great commission was addressed exclusively to ministers, but this is an error. Each church member should consider that commission as binding *him* to disciple others to the extent of his power. How affecting is the call to labor for the salvation of souls. The harvest is still plenteous and the laborers are still few.

We will first speak of efforts for the salvation of individuals. All true Christians exert themselves to some extent to further the interests of the Saviour's kingdom, but most fail to put forth personal efforts for *individuals.* And yet it is obvious to all that the kingdom of Christ can be extended in our world only by the accession of individuals. "His blood avails not to the salvation of men in the mass, but to those who individually repent of sin, and accept of His mercy. The Holy Spirit strives with men, and sanctifies them only as individuals. It is as individuals that the inhabitants of our world must be raised to heaven or sink to hell. Yet to how great an extent are the prayers of Christians offered, indefinitely for the conversion of the world as a whole, while the salvation of no one *individual* is the object of their personal and persevering endeavors."

Not merely want of zeal and of warmth of piety hinder some Christians from addressing the impenitent, but they suppose it to be a work which calls for superior talent or knowledge on the part of him who performs it, and they imagine that they are not possessed of these qualifications. They are entirely mistaken. No remarkable gift of speech is required. All one needs is to have a heart for the work, and that can be obtained. A single sentence, uttered with earnestness and feeling, has often proved an arrow from God's bow. The shipmaster who spoke to Jonah (Jonah i. 6) was probably no remarkable specimen of intelligence or talent, and yet he was able to cry, "What meanest thou, O sleeper? arise, call upon thy God." Let not the convert put off speaking to the impenitent under the impression that he lacks the needed talent. He has the gift in sufficient measure, and it is capable of being improved by use. It is also his privilege to pray for an increase of skill in addressing the unconverted.

"The church of modern times has never yet called into action one fiftieth part of the strength which it really possesses. Among its members there are hundreds, there are thousands who have done nothing for Christ. Whatever may be its cause, this silence of Christians is the undoing of thousands. It may be indolence, it may be timidity, it may be mistaken affection, it may be mere procrastination without any assignable reason, but its results are the same, and those results are tremendous beyond description. Whatever may be the piety and devotedness of ministers of the gospel the world will remain unsaved, while the conversion of sinners is left to them. To warn the sinner of the doom which awaits him, and to warn him now, while yet there remains a way of escape, is therefore the sacred obligation of all who love the Lord Jesus Christ in sincerity. It is true that not one has died in his sins but has justly perished by his own iniquity, but that is no excuse for us. The guilt of those who perish cannot justify our negligence. Every Christian must feel his own responsibility and make it one subject of his daily prayers that God would make him instrumental in winning souls. Devoted, personal, and unremitting effort on the part of the whole body of the faithful, would bring down such a blessing that there would be no room to contain it, the wilderness and the solitary place would be glad, and the desert would rejoice and blossom as the rose; churches and pastors would be doubled and quadrupled; repeated success would embolden the timid and encourage the desponding, and each new convert would immediately become a valuable auxiliary to the great cause of truth and holiness."

As this little book may fall into the hands of some new disciple, we would urge on him the importance of beginning at once to seek to save souls. Avoid everything which experience teaches you will make it difficult to address the unconverted.

Do not forget relatives while exerting yourself for others.

Be encouraged by the thought that while you are endeavoring to save others your own soul is receiving benefit.

Think of the joy of meeting those you have been the means of saving in heaven. "Your worldly labors, however unblamable, can carry no fruit into heaven. Whereas your labors in the cause of Christ are all to reappear in that day. The souls you may convert from the error of their ways, and save from death, shall be with you in heaven, and to all eternity. Faint not, therefore, but boldly face and undertake your duty in reference to this department of Christian activity."

Not only would you be honored and blessed

should you be instrumental in the conversion of souls, but the Saviour would thereby be glorified. This motive should be stronger than any other which can influence you to seek the salvation of your fellow men. Whenever a sinner is saved—saved in spite of the fearful difficulties in the way, and the opposition of Satan and all his hosts, Jesus is victorious—He is glorified, a new star is added to His crown. Perhaps our prayers and labors for the conversion of men would more frequently be blessed to their salvation, were we, in the efforts which we put forth, more influenced by the desire that our blessed Redeemer should be glorified.

Pray much that you may be successful, but do not be discouraged, should you not always succeed. Disappointment in one quarter may be counterbalanced by success in another.

Use various means. "An affectionate and faithful letter to an unconverted acquaintance is often the very message to be owned of the Spirit." But whatever means you may employ, follow up your effort by subsequent endeavors. For your encouragement remember the great usefulness which has attended the persevering exertions of many, no more gifted or fitted for the work than you are.

If you are faithful in efforts to save your fellow men, you will set an example to Christians around you which will have its effect. Even ministers may be stirred up to exertion, and make greater efforts for the souls of individuals, when they witness the activity of the Church's converts.

Seek to have an intense conviction of the truth of all that is said in the Bible, both as to the worth of the soul, and the misery of impenitent sinners. A deep conviction of the truth is necessary to strengthen your hands. Your spiritual power as a laborer must be feeble if you only half believe God's assurances, while if you believe mightily, your influence over others for God will be correspondingly great.

Remember that while God alone can give us anxiety for sinners, he *will* give us that feeling, if we sincerely desire it, and if at the same time we are making efforts to save men. It is said of a certain faithful laborer, (Harlan Page), that " his anxiety for individuals was frequently such that he could not rest, but would leave his business to seek an interview with them, or address them by letter, or pray for them. At the close of religious meetings his mind would often become intensely fixed upon the conversion of some impenitent individual. He would address him with great solemnity, urging an immediate compliance with the terms of the gospel; and as his friend accompanied him homewards, such was sometimes the pressure upon his heart, that they would seek a retired spot, and there, even in the depths of winter, kneel and plead with God, for the person's salvation." Surely this feeling of concern for others was God's gift to him, while he was in the way of duty.

Frequently seek out and converse with those who are absolutely uncared for. Go even to the outcast. "It is my rule," said a good man, "to go not only to those who need me, but to those who need me most." It is a mistake to presume that those belonging to the worst layers of society, are necessarily devoid of all thought about religion. With their sense of misery they often have a tormenting consciousness of guilt. Most truly has it been said that these abandoned ones are often lashed and stung by remorse. Go sometimes to the poor creatures, viewed, alas! by most, with loathing, and tell them that it is a faithful saying, that Christ Jesus came into the world to save sinners.

You have never been ignorant of the truth that it is faith in Jesus which is the condition of salvation. You have recently, however, known, as a matter of experience, that the great thing is to have this faith. You are prepared, therefore, to show the convinced sinner what he must do to be saved. Tell him that he is to believe on the Lord Jesus Christ. Some may have told him that submission to God is the condition. Others, that giving his heart to God is the condition. These acts of the soul are indeed duties, and they are holy acts, but neither of them is the condition of salvation. We are taught in the Bible that it is faith. And the faith which is necessary is the faith which has the blessed Saviour for its object. Tell the inquirer to trust in Jesus, to come to Him, to lay hold upon Him. This counsel proceeds on the assumption that you will (if you are really active in this work), sometimes be called to help the convinced and anxious sinner as well as warn the unawakened. " Numerous as are the ranks of the unconverted, they will most surely and rapidly disappear when once the passion for saving souls takes possession of Christ's Church on earth ; when in the warehouse and in the shop, in the factory and in the mill, in the granary and in the field, on the roadside and at the fireside, in the city and in the country, on the sea and on the shore, men and women are eagerly watching to win some soul to Christ ; when love for the world shall burn in *each* heart, prayer for the world ascend from *each* lip, bounty for the world drop from *each* hand, the messenger of mercy gush from *every* tongue. Then, O *then*, shall linger no longer the salvation of a ruined race."

Thus far we have spoken of personal efforts for the souls of individuals. But there are powerful agencies employed by the Church to advance the Saviour's kingdom, as :

Those societies which go by the names of the Foreign, and Domestic Missionary Societies.

The Bible, Tract, and Seamen's Societies.

Societies to aid Freedmen, Orphans, the wretched poor in cities, etc., etc.

The convert should at once begin to be identified with these departments of Christian activity. If he stands aloof from them at the commencement of his Christian course, the probability is that he always will. There is scarcely one who cannot do something in connection with some of these agencies. Let the convert immediately begin to read their reports and periodicals, that he may keep himself acquainted with all the work they are performing. If practicable let him offer himself to work for some of them. "The Lord prosper," says Dr. Archibald Alexander, "the self-denying company of tract distributors, who are seen penetrating into the darkest recesses of vice and infamy, bearing in their hands precious tracts, and whose lips are ever ready to pour forth, from a benevolent heart, words of exhortation, admonition, and encouragement. Let no one suppose that the missionary and the Bible supersede the necessity of tracts. These contain the very same truths which are revealed in the Bible, and it matters little how this is conveyed to the mind; if attended by the Holy Spirit, it is able to make men wise unto salvation, whether heard from the lips of a preacher, or read in an evangelical tract. Nor ought it to be objected that a large portion of the tracts and religious books which are circulated are never read, and consequently produce no effect. If one in a thousand is read with profit, there is a rich compensation for all the expense incurred."

There is no better way in which the convert can aid these agencies than by pouring out the most earnest prayers for their success and prosperity. He certainly will statedly contribute of his means to support them in their work, if he has the least spark of love for the cause of the blessed Jesus. He may also be expected to speak on their behalf whenever opportunity offers, and to try, in every other way in his power, to interest others in them.

One of the means, as has long been known, of bringing out the latent talent of young believers is the Sunday-school. It is the method of usefulness which first presents itself, when converts are brought into the Church and look around for a way to do good. Young church members have lately praised God for their salvation. " Who ought to be more full of eagerness to work in His cause, and what work can be named at once so promising, so simple, and so accessible ? The young professor who begins early, works earnestly, and continues long, actually effects, upon the successive classes that come under his care, changes which are of incalculable benefit to the land and the Church. *When he gathers a new class of poor children, and keeps them together for years, and labors for their souls*, he does more to hold up the hands of his pastor and elders, than by any and all other means which can easily be thought of. And what a propelling force does the company of young disciples give to their Church, who, after conference and prayer, fix upon a new locality, and there, in some destitute vicinage, institute a new Sunday-school."

The fact should not be concealed from the convert that, in whatever way a Christian serves Christ, the service is against nature. " He greatly errs who enters the Christian course as a career of ease, or who expects a bed of roses. From beginning to end it is against the stream. It is against the world. It is against the devil. It is against ourselves. In the natural world mountains are not ascended without many a panting effort, and many a moment of weakness; but no earthly mountains are so difficult as those we have to traverse in our spiritual march. The Christian course is a life of warfare, and of labor within and without. But, if the whole life of our adorable Lord was one bearing of the cross, surely we ought to make it the law of our existence here to bear the yoke which He lays upon us. There is such weakness in human nature, that even our most delightful duties become a burden, except so far as we receive continual supplies of grace to quicken and refresh us." Such supplies of grace, however, are promised. Moreover, the laborer who is never weary in well doing, who is always abounding in the work of the Lord, is assured by God, Himself, that he cannot labor in vain (1 Cor. xv. 58). The desire of his heart to be useful to precious souls and to the Church of God, which He purchased with His own blood, shall certainly be gratified. In addition to this, his heart is cheered by the certainty that, if he continues to serve the Master faithfully unto death, he shall be greeted with the ravishing welcome : " Well done, good and faithful servant : enter thou into the joy of thy Lord."

CHAPTER V.

FROM THE EARLIEST TIMES SPECIAL ATTENTION HAS BEEN GIVEN BY THE CHURCH TO CATECHIZING THE YOUNG.

THERE are those who are unable to remember the time when they did not love God, and trust in Jesus for their salvation. Such, in almost all cases, had faithful parents—parents who, recognizing the truth that the offspring of believers are embraced in the covenant, with tender solicitude, and many believing prayers, trained them up in the nurture and admonition of the Lord. By the very birth of this class, the Church is constantly increasing; and our plan of treatment permits us to include them, while they continue to be of tender age, among the number of converts. But, there are still others, not strictly converts—the young and ignorant who abound wherever the Church exists, and upon whom she has some hold—whom she may justly hope will become her converts with proper treatment. That to give instruction to all such, as well as to her baptized members, is the Church's duty will not be denied, nor will it be questioned that one of the methods of teaching them, which she is bound to pursue, is that of implanting in their minds the doctrines of Christianity by means of short compends and systems.

Sabbath-schools need not stand in the way of this method of instruction, nor need this doctrinal instruction interfere with the work of Sabbath-schools. The young and ignorant cannot be indoctrinated as they should be, either by Sabbath-school teaching, or by means of elaborate and continued discourses from the pulpit.

Oral instruction in a familiar way, (the pupils being sometimes required to recite what was said), was held in the highest estimation in the early Church not only as the means of instilling divine truth into the minds of converts, but for the religious teaching of those who were without the pale of the Church.

Whenever the early Church writers allude to

the catechizing which prevailed in primitive times, they use the word in the sense of initiating the ignorant in Christian rudiments, whether by question and answer or otherwise. For the method of question and answer, although closely connected with catechizing, and of great importance, is not essential to it.

Those to whose presiding care the flock was committed, felt the importance of systematically instructing by catechizing all the children of Christians, and all who applied for admission into the Church from among the heathen. A class of catechumens was attached to every church, and formed a kind of school, in which the first principles of religion were inculcated, and certain formulas of Christian doctrine were carefully committed to memory, together with portions of the sacred Scriptures. Thus, even in the beginnings of the Church's existence, she understood her vocation. She felt that her great duty was to teach. Accordingly she was, as she ought always to be, like a great school. "The κατηχούμενος" (says Dr. J. W. Alexander, "Fam. Letters," vol. 2, p. 170) "was under schooling, long watched, slowly indoctrinated." And he adds, "The Church, as a school, has declined; hence, the Sunday-school has been built up alongside."

Those who gave special instruction to the catechumens were called catechists. The catechumens embraced people of all ranks and of all grades of culture, so that it was often necessary that the teachers should be men thoroughly instructed and disciplined. At the head of the catechetical school of Alexandria, in Egypt, were men of the highest character for learning and piety. "It had at first but a single teacher, afterward, two or more, but no fixed salary or special buildings. The teachers gave their instructions in their dwellings. The first superintendent of this school known to us was Pantænus, who afterward labored as a missionary in India. He was followed by Clement to A.D. 202, and Clement by Origen to A.D. 232, who raised the school to the summit of its prosperity."

Not only did holy men of God devote much of their time to the instruction of the rising generation, and of converts from paganism, but many of the fathers felt so deeply interested in their instruction that they composed numerous treatises to be used explicitly in teaching them. The learned Dr. Coleman, in his "Antiquities of the Christian Church," gives us very interesting information in regard to the reasons which led to the institution of the order of catechumens, the age at which they were admitted, the term of instruction, the different classes into which they were divided, the mode of admission, etc. At first the purity of the Church was guarded by men who possessed the miraculous gift of discerning spirits; but, after this gift had been withdrawn, it became unsafe, immediately and as soon as they avowed their faith, to admit candidates from among the heathen into the fellowship of the Church. Multitudes who professed to be believers, when temptations and persecutions arose, went back to their former mode of life. In order to diminish, and, if possible, to prevent such apostacies, the Rulers of the Church adopted the plan of deferring the admission of converts until reasonable evidence was obtained of their fitness in point of knowledge and sincerity, to be enrolled in the ranks of the disciples. They not only continued the applicants for Church membership in a state of probation for a limited time, but they instituted schools, especially for their instruction, and appointed catechists over them. In process of time these catechetical schools became numerous, and proved of great service to the Church, and some of them became famous.

There was no specific rule respecting the age in which Jewish and heathen converts were received as catechumens. History informs us that the greater part were persons of adult age. As to the time which the catechumens should spend in that relation it varied according to the usages of the Churches. It also depended upon the proficiency of each, individually. There was no essential rule by which the converts were classified. Some writers give but two classes, others three, and others four. " The gradations of improvement were particularly observed. The age and sex and circumstances of the catechumens were also duly regarded, men of age and rank not being classed with children of twelve or thirteen years of age."

As soon as one expressed his desire and resolution to embrace the religion of Jesus, he was trained, by a regular course of catechetical instruction in private, to a knowledge of the leading doctrines and duties of the gospel; and, after this private instruction, " he was subjected to frequent and minute examinations in public on every branch of his religious education. If approved, he was forthwith instructed in some of the sublimer points of Christianity which had hitherto been withheld from him—such as the doctrine of the Trinity, the union of the divine and human natures in Christ, the influences of the Spirit, and the way in which a participation of the symbols of a Saviour's love gives spiritual nourishment to the soul. He was enjoined to commit to memory the creed as a formula, which embodied, in a small compass, all the grand articles of revealed truth, which it had been the object of his protracted discipline to teach him. For twenty successive days he continued a course of partial fasting, during which he had daily interviews with his minister, who, in private, and secluded from the presence of every other observer, endeavored, by serious discourse, to impress his mind with a sense of the important step he was about to take, and more especially prayed with him that he might be delivered from any evil spirit that had possession of his heart, and be enabled to consecrate himself a living sacrifice to God and to the Saviour. Such was the discipline of the catechumens— a discipline to which all ranks and descriptions of men, who were desirous of being admitted into the bosom of the Church, were in primitive times indiscriminately subjected."

Thus, Christ's ministers and people in the early Church fully understood and practically recognized the fact that folded sheep needed to be watched and fed; and that, in order to be prevented from straying, they needed to be imbued with sound doctrine. Classes of instruction for converts and others, after the primitive model, would doubtless be found exceedingly valuable to the Church in our own times.

During the centuries in which darkness overspread the earth, and people were deprived of the Holy Scriptures, whatever books of instruction were prepared for the ignorant, with scarcely an exception related to nothing more important than legends, rosaries, feasts, and relics. The Waldenses, however, had, during that period, their catechism, embodying, it is needless to say, nothing so trifling and worthless, but solid scriptural instruction.

If the leaders and teachers in the primitive Church, including some of the greatest minds belonging to her, held the business of catechetical instruction in the highest estimation, it was also relied upon by the Reformers of the sixteenth century as the great means of guarding and extending the truth, and of establishing the true religion in the world. They regarded the very existence of Protestantism as depending on it. They could not find words to express how their spirits were stirred within them by the prevalent ignorance, and they clearly perceived the necessity of immediately beginning the work of religiously training the young, and that, after a regular form. Nor did they soon desist from their labors. The preparation of catechisms commanded a large part of their time. The example of the first and principal reformers, Luther and Calvin, led to the composition of a multitude of catechisms by their followers. So successful were the servants of

God of the Reformation era, in spreading, in this form, the new doctrine, that the Romanists were alarmed, and were compelled, in self-defence, to resort to the same method. Were catechetical history the theme of this chapter, it would here be in place to speak of the origin of the excellent Heidelberg Catechism, which has been more extensively used than any one composed by the Reformers.

The Larger and Shorter Catechisms of the Westminster Assembly of Divines, are also recognized by a large body of Christians as containing the exact doctrines of the Reformation, as these are deduced from the Bible. "Never," says a writer, speaking of the labors of the men composing the Westminster Assembly, "were so much time and toil and learning bestowed on documents of the same compass. The Shorter Catechism, in particular, may be considered as one of the most complete and accurate summaries of divine truth ever couched in uninspired language. It consists not of arguments, but of lucid statements, and comprehensive definitions of truth, and no one who has not minutely analyzed and expounded them, can be at all aware of the logical precision, and the symmetry, and withal the seriousness and unction of these statements. The principles of moral and religious truth contained in that sublime symbol, when once embedded in the mind, enlarge, sustain, and illuminate it for all time." The Church's best and wisest teachers, both of former times and in our own day, have ever dwelt upon the importance of requiring those under a course of religious instruction to commit to memory a set form. "The popular and slovenly method is, to ask a multitude of questions to be answered in the pupil's own words. The basis of every science, however, as a subject of teaching, is laid in concise and exact definitions, and, as the language of these definitions cannot be altered without some loss, so the only safe method of beginning, is to charge the memory of the learner with the very words of such definitions. This is equally true of syntax, geometry, physics, metaphysics, and theology. The way of discovering truth is not always the way of inculcating it. All first lines of instruction must proceed upon authority; the truth must be given as dogma. In a word, though we arrive at principles analytically, we teach them synthetically. Hence, it is not a traditionary but a most philosophic method to demand the accurate learning by rote of catechetical forms."

At the regular monthly meeting of the New England Historic-Genealogical Society, held Dec. 4, 1878, a paper was read by Dr. Dorus Clarke, entitled "Saying the Catechism Seventy-five Years ago, and the Historical Results." From this paper we make the following quotation :

"I desire, in this presence, to acknowledge my deep obligations to my parents, who, long since, as I trust, 'passed into the skies,' for their fidelity in requiring me, much against my will, to commit to memory the Assembly's Catechism, and to say it six or seven years in succession in the old meeting-house in Westhampton, amid tremblings and agitations I can never cease to remember. The Catechism formed a part of the curriculum of all the *common schools* in that town for half a century, and was as thoroughly taught, and as regularly recited there, as Webster's Spelling-Book, or

Murray's English Grammar. It was as truly a classic as any other book. It was taught everywhere—in the family, in the school, and in the Church—indeed, it was the principal intellectual and religious pabulum of the people. We had it for breakfast, and we had it for dinner, and we had it for supper. The entire town was saturated with its doctrines, and it is almost as much so at the present day. The people could not, of course, descend into the profound depths of the metaphysics of theology, but they thoroughly understood the system which was held by the fathers of New England. The practice of instructing the children thoroughly in the Catechism was very general throughout New England for a century and a half after the arrival of " The Mayflower." Judge Sewall, in the first volume of his " Diary," just published by the Massachusetts Historical Society, speaks of a certain Sabbath, which, in the Old South Church in this city, was called " *The Catechising Day*," and of his wearing a new article of clothing in honor of that specially important custom. But I believe that that excellent practice was nowhere so thoroughly carried out as it was in Western Massachusetts. That was largely owing to the transcendent influence of *Jonathan Edwards—clarum et venerabile nomen*—who was looked up to by the ministers in Boston and Scotland as the oracle in all metaphysical and theological matters. His influence in Northampton and Stockbridge, and in the regions round about, is visible to-day in the peculiar moral and religious *grain* of the people. . . . . The Catechism was required, by the public sentiment of the town, to be perfectly committed to memory, and recited in the meeting-house by all the children and youth between the ages of eight and fifteen. These public recitations were held on three different Sabbaths in the summer of every year, with, perhaps, a fortnight intervening between each of them, to allow sufficient time for the children to commit to memory the division assigned. All the children in the town, dressed in their Sabbath-day clothes, were arranged shoulder to shoulder, the boys on the one side, and the girls on the other of the broad aisle—beginning at the deacon's seat beneath the pulpit, and extending down that aisle, and round through the side aisles as far as was necessary. The parents crowded the pews and galleries, tremblingly anxious that their little ones might acquit themselves well. Father Hale, standing in the pulpit, put out the questions to the children in order; and each one, when the question came to him, was expected to wheel out of the line, *à la militaire*, into the broad aisle, and face the minister, and make his very best obeisance, and answer the question put to him without the slightest mistake. To be *told*, that is, to be prompted or corrected by the minister, was not a thing to be permitted by any child who expected thereafter to have any reputation in that town for good scholarship. In this manner the three divisions of the Catechism were successively recited. . . . . This system of thorough, religious training continued through the lifetime of nearly two generations, and, therefore, long enough fairly to test its real influence upon human character and life— long enough to determine, historically, what were its legitimate effects upon individuals and upon society. I know it is difficult to ascertain precisely all the influences, open and secret, remote and proximate, which form the web and the woof of individual and municipal character; but in this case those formative factors were so immediate and so obvious, that there is little room to doubt what they were. Indeed, there is no more reason to doubt what they were, than there is to question the veracity of the multiplication table, or the excellence of the Ten Commandments. The general *result* was, and still is, that sobriety, large intelligence, sound morality, and unfeigned piety, exist there to a wider extent than in any other community of equal size within the limits of my acquaintance. Revivals of religion have been of great frequency, purity, and power; and to-day more than *one-third* of the population, all told, are members of that Congregational Church. *Nine-tenths* of the inhabitants are regular attendants on public worship. . . . I have resided in that town sixteen years, in Williamstown four years, in Andover three years, in Blandford twelve years, in Springfield six years, and in Boston and its vicinity thirty-seven years, and have therefore had some opportunities to form an intelligent judgment of the relative condition, moral and religious, of different parts of this Commonwealth; and I say it 'without fear or favor, or hope of reward;' I say it with no invidious spirit whatever; I say it simply because historic verity peremptorily requires that it *should* be said— that I have nowhere found, in these communities generally, such profound reverence for the name of JEHOVAH, the Infinite and Personal GOD; such unquestioning faith in the divine authority of the Holy Scriptures; such devout and conscientious observance of the Sabbath; such habitual practice of family prayer; such respect for an oath in a court of justice; such anxiety for revivals of religion; such serious determination to enter into the kingdom of heaven; and such deep conviction that it never can be reached, except by repentance for sin, and faith in a crucified Redeemer, as I have seen in that town. That the moral and religious condition of things there is not what it should be, is unquestionably true; but that it is, on the whole, better, yes, much better, than that in any other municipality on the face of the earth, which has not been similarly educated, is my honest belief. And, if this be true, this superior Christian tone of society must have had an adequate cause ; and it is our duty, as members of this Historical Society, to ascertain that cause, and let it be known for the information and imitation of the world. That cause—so far as I am able to trace effects back to their causes—can be found, not in the local position of that town, not in its scenery, not in its peculiarly favorable situation for the prosecution of any of the arts of life, not in the wealth created by great manufacturing industries, but in its more thorough indoctrination, from its settlement down to the present day, in the great truths of the Bible, creating public sentiment, permeating domestic life, giving vigor to conscience, converting men to Christ, and impregnating society, through all its ramifications, with a profounder sense of moral obligation."

The Catechism is now made in our Church a part of the *curriculum* of Sabbath-school instruction, and this is well, provided it is also recited at other times than in the Sabbath-school, To commit it to memory without incessantly reviewing it, is not to become sufficiently familiar with it. In order that its definitions may make the deepest impression on the mind, they must be repeated again and again, and that with punctilious accuracy through a long series of years. It is only thus that the great truths of the Catechism can be deeply "imbedded" in our children's minds, or wrought, as it were, into their very texture. It is absurd to object to the accurate learning of catechetical forms by rote. Who will pretend to deny the truth of the statement of the writer just now quoted, that *All first lines of instruction must proceed upon authority?* But we shall not pursue the subject further, as to give the history of catechizing is no part of the purpose of this little book.

The ignorant and uncared for, abound wherever the Church is planted, and there is a sense in which they all belong to her.* They belong

---

* It is very much owing to the unfaithfulness of God's people that the number of persons ignorant of the teachings of the Bible, though living in Christian communities, is so great. Those who have read the account given by Dr. Spencer, in his "Pastor's Sketches," of the conversion, on her death-bed, of the Welsh woman's young tenant, may remember how feelingly he

to her to instruct and train for heaven. This has been assumed in what has been said in this concluding chapter. But it is chiefly for the purpose of enlisting sympathy and aid in behalf of converts, that these pages have been written. We have seen that there are many encouragements to engage in the work of aiding them. The number of new disciples in the world is at all times very great. Perhaps an hour does not pass in which souls somewhere are not regenerated by the Holy Spirit. It is astonishing that these are not more cared for by God's people. To guard, cherish, and feed them is one of the ends for which the Church has been organized.

---

deplores the shocking unfaithfulness to this young woman's soul, of those who had been long her intimate associates. "What a lesson of reproof to Christians," he says, "that this woman, living for twenty years among them, and in the sight of five or six Christian churches, should never have been inside of a church in her life, and that nobody asked her to go. Year after year she was in habits of intimacy with those who belonged in Christian families; she associated with children of Christian parents and yet she had never read the Bible—she never was exhorted to seek the Lord! And probably she would have died as she had lived had not divine Providence sent her to be the tenant of the 'old lady' who loved her so well."

Christ has not only enjoined it upon His Church to disciple all nations, but to make His converts, whom He so much loves, worthy, and strong, and useful disciples. No plan employed by the Church to make them such, however wisely devised, can be of the least avail, unless believers, as individuals, feel a deeper interest in them and exert themselves more for their good. What can be of greater importance to converts than that they should start aright. May it not be truthfully said of most of them that they will be through life, what they are during their first months of profession. "The conversion of a man is only the first step in a heavenly course—is only the entrance at the wicket gate, as Bunyan puts it, with all the difficulties, perils, and conflicts of the pilgrimage itself yet before him." Remember that a powerful means of benefiting converts is to pray for them. Intercede for them, therefore, daily during the remainder of your life.

Old Faiths in New Light

BY

NEWMAN SMYTH,

Author of "The Religious Feeling."

One Volume, 12mo, cloth, - - - $1.50.

This work aims to meet a growing need by gathering materials of faith which have been quarried by many specialists in their own departments of Biblical study and scientific research, and by endeavoring to put these results of recent scholarship together according to one leading idea in a modern construction of old faith. Mr. Smyth's book is remarkable no less for its learning and wide acquaintance with prevailing modes of thought, than for its fairness and judicial spirit.

CRITICAL NOTICES.

"The author is logical and therefore clear. He also is master of a singularly attractive literary style. Few writers, whose books come under our eye, succeed in treating metaphysical and philosophical themes in a manner at once so forcible and so interesting. We speak strongly about this book, because we think it exceptionally valuable. It is just such a book as ought to be in the hands of all intelligent men and women who have received an education sufficient to enable them to read intelligently about such subjects as are discussed herein, and the number of such persons is very much larger than some people think."—*Congregationalist.*

"We have before had occasion to notice the force and elegance of this writer, and his new book shows scholarship even more advanced. * * * When we say, with some knowledge of how much is undertaken by the saying, that there is probably no book of moderate compass which combines in greater degree clearness of style with profundity of subject and of reasoning, we fulfil simple duty to an author whose success is all the more marked and gratifying from the multitude of kindred attempts with which we have been flooded from all sorts of pens."—*Presbyterian.*

"The book impresses us as clear, cogent and helpful, as vigorous in style as it is honest in purpose, and calculated to render valuable service in showing that religion and science are not antagonists but allies, and that both lead up toward the one God. We fancy that a good many readers of this volume will entertain toward the author a feeling of sincere personal gratitude."—*Boston Journal.*

"On the whole, we do not know of a book which may better be commended to thoughtful persons whose minds have been unsettled by objections of modern thought. It will be found a wholesome work for every minister in the land to read."
—*Examiner and Chronicle.*

"It is a long time since we have met with an abler or fresher theological treatise than *Old Faiths in New Light*, by Newman Smyth, an author who in his work on "The Religious Feeling" has already shown ability as an expounder of Christian doctrine."—*Independent.*

** *For sale by all booksellers, or sent postpaid, upon receipt of price, by*

CHARLES SCRIBNER'S SONS,

Nos. 743 AND 745 BROADWAY, NEW YORK.

Gates Into the Psalm-Country

BY

Rev. MARVIN R. VINCENT, D.D.

One Volume, 12mo, - - - - - - $1.50.

CRITICAL NOTICES.

"The book may be cordially recommended to the perusal of young men especially, who will find in it the soundest views of life and the most elevated religious conceptions, enforced with equal kindness, eloquence, and power."—*New York Tribune.*

"As meditations upon that portion of Scripture designed for popular rather than critical reading, they are delightful. The thought is warm and earnest, and, like the Psalms themselves, these studies suggested by them deal with the common experiences of life."—*The Churchman.*

"In the execution of his design, Dr. Vincent has shown rare skill and ability. The work seems to us to be a model of its kind—scholarly, thoughtful, enriched but not encumbered by the results of the best learning, devout and cheerful in spirit, practical, sensible, and like the Psalms themselves, full of Christ and the Gospel. The style is singularly clear, racy, and incisive."—*New York Evangelist.*

"They are rich in spiritual counsel, graceful in style, happy in thought and illustration. The book is meant for the average Bible-reader, rather than for the scholar, and any devout Christian loving the Bible, will find in it an abundance of interesting and suggestive thought."—*Boston Watchman.*

"The treatment is deeply spiritual, the tone affectionate and earnest, and the style clear, direct, and often picturesque; and we are sure that many a Christian will find in the volume both instruction and solace, and varying helps for varying times of need."—*Boston Congregationalist.*

"They who thoughtfully read these pages find themselves not only illumined and refreshed by the immediate subject, but stimulated to make the Psalter fruitful under their own meditative study."
—*New York Christian Intelligencer.*

"Like the different parts of a beautiful garden, or the successive strains of sweet music, these discourses charm the soul and fill it with rupturous emotions. They are at the same time most helpful in the way of right living."—*Lutheran Quarterly.*

"Christians of every name will find strength and comfort in these essays, which are as sweet as they are simple, and as solid as they are unpretentious."—*The Living Church.*

⁎⁎⁎ For sale by all booksellers, or will be sent, prepaid, upon receipt of price by

CHARLES SCRIBNER'S SONS,
Nos. 743 and 745 Broadway, New York.

The Conflict of Christianity
WITH HEATHENISM.
By DR. GERHARD UHLHORN.
TRANSLATED BY
PROF. EGBERT C. SMYTH and REV. C. J. H. ROPES.

One Volume, Crown 8vo, $2.50.

This volume describes with extraordinary vividness and spirit the religious and moral condition of the Pagan world, the rise and spread of Christianity, its conflict with heathenism, and its final victory. There is no work that portrays the heroic age of the ancient church with equal spirit, elegance, and incisive power. The author has made thorough and independent study both of the early Christian literature and also of the contemporary records of classic heathenism.

CRITICAL NOTICES.

"It is easy to see why this volume is so highly esteemed. It is systematic, thorough, and concise. But its power is in the wide mental vision and well-balanced imagination of the author, which enable him to reconstruct the scenes of ancient history. An exceptional clearness and force mark his style."—*Boston Advertiser.*

"One might read many books without obtaining more than a fraction of the profitable information here conveyed; and he might search a long time before finding one which would so thoroughly fix his attention and command his interest."—*Phil. S. S. Times.*

"Dr. Uhlhorn has described the great conflict with the power of a master. His style is strong and attractive, his descriptions vivid and graphic, his illustrations highly colored, and his presentation of the subject earnest and effective."—*Providence Journal.*

"The work is marked for its broad humanitarian views, its learning, and the wide discretion in selecting from the great field the points of deepest interest."—*Chicago Inter-Ocean.*

"This is one of those clear, strong, thorough-going books which are a scholar's delight."—*Hartford Religious Herald.*

*** For sale by all booksellers, or sent post-paid upon receipt of price, by

CHARLES SCRIBNER'S SONS,
Nos. 743 AND 745 BROADWAY, NEW YORK.

Faith and Rationalism.

By Prof. GEORGE P. FISHER, D.D.,
Author of "The Beginnings of Christianity," "The Reformation," Etc.

One Volume, 12mo. Cloth, $1.25.

"This valuable and timely volume discusses ably, trenchantly and decisively the subjects of which it treats. It contains within small limits a large amount of information and unanswerable reasoning."—*Presbyterian Banner.*

"The book is valuable as a discussion of the mysteries of faith and the characteristics of rationalism by one of the clearest writers and thinkers."—*Washington Post.*

"The author deals with many of the questions of the day, and does so with a freshness and completeness quite admirable and attractive."—*Presbyterian.*

"This singularly clear and catholic-spirited essay will command the attention of the theological world, for it is a searching inquiry into the very substance of Christian belief."—*Hartford Courant.*

"This little volume may be regarded as virtually a primer of modern religious thought, which contains within its condensed pages rich materials that are not easily gathered from the great volumes of our theological authors. Alike in learning, style and power of descrimination, it is honorable to the author and to his university, which does not urge the claims of science by slighting the worth of faith or philosophy."—*N. Y. Times.*

"Topics of profound interest to the studious inquirer after truth are discussed by the author with his characteristic breadth of view, catholicity of judgment, affluence of learning, felicity of illustration, and force of reasoning. . . . His singular candor disarms the prepossessions of his opponents. . . . In these days of pretentious, shallow and garrulous scholarship, his learning is as noticeable for its solidity as for its compass."—*N. Y. Tribune.*

*** *The above book for sale by all booksellers, or will be sent, prepaid, upon receipt of price, by*

CHARLES SCRIBNER'S SONS, PUBLISHERS,

743 AND 745 BROADWAY, NEW YORK.

[Complete in Twenty-four Volumes 8vo.

Lange's Commentary,
CRITICAL, DOCTRINAL, AND HOMILETICAL.
TRANSLATED, ENLARGED, AND EDITED
BY
PHILIP SCHAFF, D.D.,
PROFESSOR IN THE UNION THEOLOGICAL SEMINARY.

This is the most comprehensive and exhaustive Commentary on the whole Bible ever published in this or any other country.

The German work, on which the English edition is based, is the product of about twenty distinguished Biblical scholars, of Germany, Holland, and Switzerland, and enjoys a high reputation and popularity wherever German theology is studied.

The American edition is not a mere translation (although embracing the whole of the German), but, to a large extent, an *original* work; about one-third of the matter being added, and the whole adapted to the wants of the English and American student. Its popularity and sale has been lately increasing in Great Britain.

The press has been almost unanimous in its commendation of LANGE'S COMMENTARY. It is generally regarded as being, on the whole, the most useful Commentary, especially for ministers and theological students—in which they are more likely to find what they desire than in any other. It is a complete treasury of Biblical knowledge, brought down to the latest date. It gives the results of careful, scholarly research; yet in a form sufficiently popular for the use of intelligent laymen. The Homiletical department contains the best thoughts of the great divines and pulpit orators of all ages, on the texts explained, and supplies rich suggestions for sermons and Bible lectures.

The following are some of the chief merits of this Commentary:

1. *It is orthodox and sound*, without being sectarian or denominational. It fairly represents the exegetical and doctrinal *consensus* of evangelical divines of the present age, and yet ignores none of the just claims of liberal scientific criticism.

2. *It is comprehensive and complete*—giving in beautiful order the authorized English version with emendations, a digest of the Critical Apparatus, Exegetical Explanations, Doctrinal and Ethical Inferences and Reflections, and Homiletical and Practical Hints and Applications.

3. *It is the product of fifty American (besides twenty European) Scholars*, from the leading denominations and Theological institutions of the country. Professors in the Theological Seminaries of New York, Princeton, Andover, New Haven, Hartford, Cambridge, Rochester, Philadelphia, Cincinnati, Alleghany, Chicago, Madison, and other places, representing the Presbyterian, Episcopal, Congregational, Baptist, Methodist, Lutheran, and Reformed Churches, have contributed to this Commentary, and enriched it with the results of their special studies. It may, therefore, claim a national character more than any other work of the kind ever published in this country.

8vo, per vol., in sheep, $6.50; in half calf, $7.50; cloth, $5.00.

₀ *The above book for sale by all booksellers, or will be sent, post or express charges paid, upon receipt of the price by the publishers,*

CHARLES SCRIBNER'S SONS,
743 AND 745 BROADWAY, NEW YORK

THE BIBLE COMMENTARY

The Holy Bible,

ACCORDING TO THE AUTHORIZED VERSION, A.D. 1611.
With an Explanatory and Critical Commentary, and a Revision of the Translation.

Now Ready. Complete in 6 vols. Royal 8vo. Cloth, $5.

THE OLD TESTAMENT.
Edited by F. C. COOK, M.A., Canon of Exeter, Preacher at Lincoln's Inn, and Chaplain in Ordinary to the Queen.

VOL.   I.—GENESIS, EXODUS, LEVITICUS, NUMBERS, DEUTERONOMY.
VOL. II.—JOSHUA, JUDGES, RUTH, SAMUEL, 1st KINGS.
VOL. III.—2d KINGS, CHRONICLES, EZRA, NEHEMIAH, ESTHER.
VOL. IV.—JOB, PSALMS, PROVERBS, ECCLESIASTES, SONG OF SOLOMON.
VOL.   V.—ISAIAH, JEREMIAH, LAMENTATIONS.
VOL. VI.—EZEKIEL, DANIEL, THE MINOR PROPHETS.

The want of a plain, Explanatory COMMENTARY ON THE BIBLE more complete and accurate than any accessible to English readers having been long felt by men of education, in 1863 the SPEAKER OF THE HOUSE OF COMMONS consulted some of the the Bishops as to the best way of supplying the deficiency; and the ARCHBISHOP OF YORK undertook to organize a plan for producing such a work, by the co-operation of scholars selected for their biblical learning.

The great object of this Commentary, of which the Old Testament is now completed, is to put the general reader in full possession of whatever information may be requisite to enable him to understand the Holy Scriptures, to give him, as far as possible, the same advantages as the scholar, and to supply him with satisfactory answers to objections resting upon misrepresentations of the text.

It was decided to reprint, without alteration, the Authorized Version from the edition of 1611, with the marginal references and renderings. Special care has been taken to furnish in all cases amended translations of passages proved to be incorrect in our version. The Comment is chiefly explanatory, presenting, in a concise and readable form, the results of learned investigations, carried on in this and other countries during the last half century. When fuller discussions of difficult passages or important subjects are necessary, they are placed at the end of the chapter, or of the volume.

The conduct of the work—as general Editor—has been entrusted to the Rev. F. C. Cook, M.A., Canon of Exeter, Preacher at Lincoln's Inn, and Chaplain in Ordinary to the Queen.

The Archbishop of York, in consultation with the Regius Professors of Divinity of Oxford and Cambridge, advises with the general Editor upon questions arising during the progress of the work.

IN THE PRESS.
THE NEW TESTAMENT.

VOL.   I.—MATTHEW, MARK, and LUKE. *(Now Ready.)*
VOL. II.—JOHN and ACTS. *(Now Ready.)*
VOL. III.—EPISTLES OF ST. PAUL.
VOL. IV.—CATHOLIC EPISTLES AND REVELATIONS.

*** *The above books for sale by all booksellers, or will be sent, post or express charges paid, upon receipt of the price by the publishers,*

CHARLES SCRIBNER'S SONS,
743 AND 745 BROADWAY, NEW YORK

www.ingramcontent.com/pod-product-compliance
Lightning Source LLC
Chambersburg PA
CBHW020242170426
43202CB00008B/194